WAYBREAD

MEMORIES OF THE CAMINO FOR THE ONWARD JOURNEY

LAURIE DENNETT

PEACEABLE PUBLISHING

ISBN: 978-0-9855032-5-3
First printing, 2023.

Peaceable Publishing, Moratinos, Palencia Spain
& Vandergrift, Pennsylvania USA

For Don Elias Valiña,
and for those he inspired
to 'keep the Camino, camino'

CONTENTS

How is a pilgrim like a blacksmith?
He bends iron. Love bends him.
- Anne Carson

'The Anthropology of Water',
in *Plainwater. Essays and Poetry*. (New York, 1995). p. 176.

Publisher's Note:

Thousands of English-speaking people fall under the spell of the Camino de Santiago every year, captured in its net of spirituality, welcome, legend, ritual, and generosity. Some of them decide to dive deeper into the philosophy, history, and spirit that gave rise to the Camino phenomenon.

Tantalizing questions come up:

If St James's body is in Santiago, how did his hand get to England? Can you still go and see it?

What kind of welcome did a pilgrim get in Rabanal del Camino in 1986? How did pilgrims in those days get trail information before the internet made it so easy?

How "Christian" is the Camino, really? When did pilgrims start using credentials? And what about the Compostela certificate?

Which of the old buildings in O Cebreiro was the "Hospederia" where the priest Don Elias Valiña Sampedro worked to create the Camino as we know it? What was that village like before the Camino came alive again? Who served the pilgrims during its thousand years of history?

Who was Don Elias? Who was the first volunteer hospitalero? Who came up with the donation-based albergue idea?

Questions come up. Answers are out there, but often only for those who read Spanish.

A huge amount of Camino lore has never been translated into English. And now, many of the people who created the present Camino are passing away, taking their stories with them.

Waybread author Laurie Dennett is one of those walking, talking treasures. She is a pilgrim, a historian, a writer, speaker, and activist. She's been studying the Way for more than 30 years, but unlike many academics she hasn't limited herself to lectures, research, and endless repeat hikes. Laurie is a doer, a motivator, a leader. She served on boards, raised funds, wrote newsletters. And when she came back to the Camino, she went to one place in particular: the Hospederia in O Cebreiro, where a small family circle worked with Don Elias to make his vision reality.

Laurie knew Don Elias well during the final phase of his life. She was part of the team from England and El Bierzo that created Refugio Gaucelmo, a pilgrim shelter in a mountain village patterned after Don Elias' oasis. She knew the Germans, Swiss, and Italians who opened a series of albergues all down the Way. She saw the rise of regional and national Camino Associations, and served as Chairman of one of the largest foreign groups – the Confraternity of St James in the United Kingdom.

She continues to write and lecture on pilgrimage history and culture at gatherings all over the Camino world.

In 2023, the time is ripe for Laurie's archive of memory and experience to come to light, in her native language. Here are sweeping histories, arcane footnotes, historic fragments, artifacts of bygone days – even notes from a 1996 committee concerned that with pilgrim numbers topping 100,000 per year, the Camino was becoming overrun and commercialized!

It is helpful – and fun – to note the dates when each item was produced, and contrast the outlook of that time with what we see on The Way today. There's a note of sweetness and collegiality from those volunteer-powered days that rings sharp against today's reality: the Camino has become a multimillion-euro business that's increasingly left to "hospitality professionals" to manage.

This is not another Camino guidebook stuffed with tall tales from the tourist office, nor another windy trail diary. This is history. It is the story of the trail itself, and the generous souls who made it transitable again after years of oblivion. It's the tale of those who still strive to keep the Camino simple, within the reach of every pilgrim who wants to walk.

This is a little garden of wisdom, study, and observation, offered in the same spirit of generosity you'll find at a donativo albergue, or a boxwood labyrinth planted on a Galician hillside. It is open to all.

Welcome, pilgrim.

Rebekah Scott
Peaceable Publishing Inc.
Moratinos, Palencia Spain

Introduction: An assortment of Writings – but Why Call it 'Waybread'?

On 1 March 2020, I left my house near O Cebreiro in Spain's autonomous region of Galicia, took the night bus to Madrid, and from there flew to my native city of Toronto for what was intended to be a two-week visit. On the news screens at Barajas airport, as on television during the previous week, reports of a viral infection originating in China and now present in a number of countries, including Spain, caught peoples' interest, but as yet did not arouse alarm. I eventually headed for my gate and thought no more about it.

Like everyone's plans, mine were turned upside-down by the extraordinary events of the next ten days. Within a week, the global spread of the virus had eclipsed all other news. The World Health Organisation issued a statement on 11 March declaring that the infection's speed and ease of transmission did indeed justify calling this a pandemic. By 13th March the world was closing down. As one country after another, Spain and Canada among them, declared states of emergency, international travel ground to a halt. Galician friends cautioned me to stay where I was if I possibly could, but within hours there was no longer any room for choice in the matter. I was well and truly stuck.

Everyone will have his or her own story of adapting to life under the uncertainties and restrictions of the months that followed. My situation was unremarkable, even fortunate, compared to many, as I recognised at the time. Far more worrying was the thought of the impact of events on friends around the world, on the part of Spain where I live, and particularly, on the Caminos de Santiago and the pilgrims whose journeys had been suddenly cut short. With albergues and hotels, shops and bars forced to close, transport cancelled and movement restricted, how were they to make their way to the towns and airports from which, in theory, they could return home? Working alongside local authorities and embassies in Spain, a network of Camino-related associations provided guidance and practical help. Thanks to all this conjoined effort, the majority of pilgrims caught out by the pandemic were able to get back to their own countries, though the journeys of some were adventurous, to say the least. Their stories, from the most harrowing to the most uplifting, are still emerging to astonish us all.

As my own weeks of lockdown turned into months, I scanned the news from Spain every morning on an erratically functioning iPad. It wasn't always easy to discern what was happening, even on my local stretch of the Camino Francés. After seventeen weeks (the same length of time, I reflected ruefully, as it had taken me to walk from Canterbury to Jerusalem back in 1992), there came a brief period when it seemed the worst had passed, and travel restrictions eased. On 8 July I was able to fly back to Madrid and make my way home to La Laguna, where the land surrounding my house was no longer a garden, but a savannah of waist-high grass and weeds.

Back in Toronto, I'd understood that the Caminos were gradually reopening, but the truce that allowed me to return to Spain was brief. With the renewal of lockdown, regional and provincial boundaries closed. Eventually I paid a neighbour to bring his tractor into the garden and cut the worst of the long grass, but weeding the flower beds was a job that could only be done by hand. I spent weeks at it, falling into bed exhausted every night, but considering myself lucky to have a well-stocked larder and freezer.

When at last, sometime in August, I took a break to drive cautiously up to O Cebreiro, I found a ghost town in all but name. There were no pilgrims, no tables or welcoming signboard menus. The church, albergue, bars and guesthouses were firmly shut, the single street empty and silent. I stood astonished, gazing around me in disbelief. I imagined that this was what hundreds of places along the Caminos must look and feel like, yet somehow, to see O Cebreiro - the cradle of the modern revival of the pilgrimage, and an obligatory pilgrim halt for more than a millennium – reduced to such a state was worse.

Or perhaps it seemed so because of the place this tiny spot has had in my heart for more than 30 years. O Cebreiro has been one fixed point of a triangular life, the other two being Toronto and London, since 1989. This is the village that had given me an extended family and a second language, some dear friendships and the inspiration for some of my best writing. When I first knew it, the modern revival of the pilgrimage was just beginning. Since the mid-1990s, however, O Cebreiro's popularity has all but eclipsed its identity. Summer mornings normally find it buzzing with pilgrims preparing to set off, calling to one another, tightening the straps on rucksacks and panniers. I'd seen it that way countless times, just as I'd known it blanketed with snow in the January dusk, with lighted windows and woodsmoke on the air. Now the walled enclosure in front of the church and the former *Meson San Giraldo de Aurillac* lay empty, with no lights anywhere. Memories scrolled through my mind, as if on a cinema screen – and faces, too. It was probably just as well there was nobody about, since I found myself so overcome by emotion that I'd have been incapable of speech. If I inwardly directed my thoughts to anyone, it was to Don Elias Valiña, whose image presides over this space in the form of a bronze bust mounted on a stone plinth, but whose absence, even after 30 years, is still so tangible as to be itself a presence.

* * *

Six months on from that silent evening in O Cebreiro, it is February 2021, and a compostellan Holy Year. In Spain, the pandemic's dreaded 'second wave' has brought heavier restrictions, a national curfew and a blanket ban on non-essential travel. The long haul through the winter has seen the Caminos forced even deeper into hibernation. Only one pilgrim, to my knowledge, has passed this way: the redoubtable Ursula Martin, on the last stage of her journey on foot from Kyiv to Santiago, before heading for home in Wales.

The monument to Don Elias Valiña Sampedro
in O Cebreiro

With the creation of vaccines, hopes are rising that the Caminos will revive soon, but it is clear that programmes of mass vaccination are still months away, and that the recovery of confidence in the safety of the routes will be the key to their re-opening. In the light of all the uncertainty, the Confraternity of Saint James's Rabanal committee, of which I am a member, has decided that Refugio Gaucelmo, the albergue we administer in Rabanal del Camino, León, should remain closed this season. As I read the emergency health measures hastily put together by the various regional authorities, applicable to every kind of accommodation from 5-star hotels to the humblest bar, I wonder whether pilgrim albergues, especially the traditional, donation-based ones like Refugio Gaucelmo, will receive any help with the cost of implementing them. I am also surprised by the tone of some of these documents. Legal pronouncements are not meant to be fun, but some of the ones I've read have been downright harsh, full of complicated citations and threats of penalties for non-compliance. The framers of such missives seem to regard the volunteers and associations of 'Amigos del Camino' in the same light as commercial entities, rather than as allies in the common cause of ensuring pilgrim safety. Ordinarily this might have struck me as merely 'typical of the politicos', but in the context of the pandemic this seems a lame excuse. Whether the authorities realise it or not, putting these new safety measures into practice will depend largely on the efforts of those dedicated people. The hectoring tone is woefully out of step with that reality, and makes me wonder how much the town hall officials really know about the Caminos they claim to take such an interest in.

* * *

Another six months have gone by, and it is August again. The Camino Francés – at least the Galician section of it – seems to be recovering much of its former activity. Now that restrictions have eased, I see pilgrims once again strung out along the road in the mornings when I drive down to Pedrafita. I raise a friendly hand to them, especially to those walking alone, as drivers once waved to me as I made my way across Spain back in 1986. In O Cebreiro, the bars and restaurants can now function at half-capacity, and pilgrims are once again permitted to sit at well-spaced tables outside and chat with one another. Day by day they are increasing in number, and I am glad to see this challenging Holy Year finally gaining some momentum.

It is heartening, too, that the isolation and restrictions of the past 18 months have not kept pilgrims from thinking, reading and talking about the Caminos, especially online, where 'virtual' book clubs and meeting places quickly sprang up around the world. Living, as I do, in a hamlet with only nine residents, and at best a precarious internet connection, I've done more reading than talking. Skimming through Elias Valiña's tiny, handmade *Boletín*, produced in the 1980s, along with back issues of the Confraternity's *Bulletin*, and *Peregrino*, the magazine of the Spanish federation of Camino-related associations, has proved an enjoyable pastime when I've had enough of pulling weeds.

It was also an instructive and useful one, because reviewing the early stages of the Camino's modern renaissance affirmed what

I've been uneasily aware of for a long time: the degree to which, in tandem with the growing emphasis on tourism, the pilgrimage has become commodified. This is hardly surprising, given the tremendous touristic promotion leading up to the 1993 and 1999 Holy Years. Even so, during the 1990s there was still a sense that the traditional pilgrimage was holding its own – that is, that the pilgrim journey on foot, bike or horseback was still generally deemed to be 'the authentic' one, motivated by personal, often existential, inquiry, in a spirit of openness and a willingness to forgo many of the comforts and distractions of everyday life.

That was, of course, before the mobile phone, the internet and wifi became ubiquitous, before GPSs and booking apps eliminated any shadow of uncertainty from the daily trek, and rucksack delivery services much of the weariness. One of the most salutary of the Camino's lessons used to be learning to distinguish essential kit from caprice, simply by carrying one's own belongings. The challenges inherent in travelling the Caminos were salutary, too, since dealing with them built confidence, ingenuity, resilience and physical wellbeing. In contrast, the aim of most of the conveniences that have arisen in response to mass tourism seems to be to render the Camino traveller self-sufficient: someone who never needs to ask for anything, and certainly one who never need suffer thirst, doubt or surprise. If the tourist-pilgrim never needs or has to ask for anything, he has little chance to test his own mettle, and he may never have occasion to meet local people – the spontaneous encounters that so often lead to what some call 'the workings of providence', whose aliases are 'chance', 'coincidence', 'serendipity', and 'random acts of kindness'. Regardless of the names they go by, such encounters have always been an integral part of the pilgrim's journey, and a large part of what makes it memorable.

Reflecting on all this, I sense that – pandemic or no pandemic – the pilgrimage, especially along the Camino Francés, is on the horns of a dilemma. One 'horn' represents the traditional pilgrimage, sustained through the centuries by ideals of hospitality. The other represents the promotion of the routes for mass tourism. Since the millennium, safeguarding the essence of the Camino ('guardamos el Camino, camino', as Elias Valiña urged us to do, back in 1987), has become increasingly difficult, since exploiting its economic potential has become a political objective. Life itself has become more complicated, especially technologically. International promotion has given rise to facilities and infrastructure to cater for annual numbers of Camino travellers that would once have been inconceivable. At the same time, local politics and the broadening interests of those same travellers have created new ways to Santiago that owe little, if anything, to historical evidence.

To be fair, the phenomenon of Camino tourism has done far too much good for anyone to wish to turn back the clock. It has lifted many rural parts of Spain out of poverty, provided employment and economic stability, highlighted the country's cultural treasures, and enriched thousands of lives. That has been my reasoning over the years, along with the view that the use of technology and conveniences were matters of personal choice. In that these made the Caminos more accessible and inclusive, that too, I thought, was surely commendable.

Yet what I observe of late is that promotion, for all its benefits, has become so dominant as to threaten the nature of the very phenomenon that gave rise to it. Here in Spain, concern about this has already found expression in the Fraternidad Internacional del Camino de Santiago (FICS, formed in 2015), an international association of volunteers that cites the example of Elias Valiña as its founding principle. So far, four municipalities have entrusted it with the running of their albergues, on a 'donativo' basis, staffed by volunteer hospitaleros. Similarly, the Asociacion de Albergues de Acogida Tradicional, founded in 2018 by some 16 donativo-based albergues, has recently proposed to UNESCO that the traditional hospitality of Spain's pilgrim roads be formally included in the cultural Patrimony of Humanity.

The fact that the collective memory of the 1980s Camino revival is fading, as those responsible for it pass away, may be inevitable, but that is only part of what associations like the FICS and the AAAC are up against. The real threat to the traditional values and quality of the pilgrimage comes, first, from regional authorities determined to ignore them, in favour of the economic and political advantages to be gained through unbridled tourism, and secondly, from some of those who have invested in Camino infrastructure (often having received grants from public funds) and now make a living through businesses set up to cater to pilgrims. Many such people have been pilgrims themselves, and are motivated by love of the Camino and a genuine desire to serve. They operate as committed members of a pluralistic Camino community, and their albergues have done much to broaden the range of people who can make the pilgrimage.

Lamentably, there are others for whom the offering of traditional hospitality to pilgrims on the part of voluntary, non-profit or charitable entities is seen as 'unfair competition', which they seek to eliminate by clamouring for discriminatory legislation, as in the autonomous region of Castile and León. An awareness that running a business involves an element of risk, and an acceptance that vast numbers of pilgrims need a corresponding variety of facilities, seems lacking here. Pilgrims who use 'donativo' albergues do so for one of two reasons: either because they prefer the simplicity, personal contact and historical resonance of the traditional model, or because they are on a tight budget. They are not, on the whole, prospective clients for private facilities, so the mentality that resents what is offered to them by others is somewhat hard to fathom. That altruistically-offered hospitality – an intrinsic part of the pilgrimage for more than a millennium – is being forced onto the defensive by an element seeking its own economic advantage suggests — at least to me — an abysmal ignorance of Camino history, equalled in depth only by a most un-Camino-like degree of selfishness.

What kind of experience are post-pandemic pilgrims going to have, and will the pilgrimage remain accessible to all, given the likelihood of increased costs and social pressures of every kind? Even my most inveterate fellow-optimists are now concerned about this. There must be some kind of conjoined effort to ensure that there is still a place for pilgrims who seek silence and relative austerity, and that making the pilgrimage does not become exclusively a pastime for the better-off. When even the Xunta de Galicia's albergues (now administered by a company owned by the businessman-president of

Real Madrid) charge eight euros per bed, most private ones between twelve and twenty euros, and even the most modest hotels anything from 40 and upwards, there is a real danger of this. The long-distance journey on foot, even if only from the Pyrenees, may soon become unaffordable for many.

Also to be feared is an increase in tensions between the owners of private facilities and those providing donativo-based beds to pilgrims, some of whom cannot afford anything else. I already know of one town where a tacit agreement ensures that the municipal albergue does not open until the private facilities are full. Then there is the question of over-promotion: in Galicia there are often more pilgrims than beds, yet the local resident who puts up a bedless pilgrim (or even a family friend) now risks being denounced for 'letting unauthorised rooms'. I know of such instances, and of another in which a group of so-called 'pilgrims' physically threatened a parish priest when he refused their demand to let them sleep in the church. All this suggests that in some Camino halts, commercialisation on one hand and over-promotion on the other now menace the very ethos that has sustained the pilgrimage through the centuries and fuelled its modern resurgence. Adding to my concern was the experience of watching a video in, of all places, the Museum of the Pilgrimages in Santiago, in which credit for the modern-day resurgence of the pilgrimage is attributed almost exclusively to politicians. The crucial role of the Camino pioneers of the 1960s and 70s, the work of the associations they founded, the parishes and people of the pilgrimage roads...none of these received so much as a mention.

To anyone who knows and loves the pilgrimage, the need to resist these disturbing trends is obvious, but for a long time I could not see any personal, constructive way of doing so. The glimmer of an idea emerged from the 'lockdown summer' of 2020. It was, as I've described, largely spent weeding. What had in happier times been a strawberry bed and a vegetable plot presented me with an array of weeds I knew, along with some new ones. That was how I became acquainted with a little plant whose refusal to be banished was exasperating: I would yank it out, but it would be soon be back, in the same spot or very nearby, probably because I had left bits of root behind. I had no idea what the plant was, but out of curiosity I photographed it and went online, where I soon found some basic information about it.

For a start, I learned that its botanical name was *Plantago major*, the broadleaf plantain, whose name in Old English was *wegbrade*, or 'waybread'. It is so common as to go unnoticed, though once you know what it looks like, you see it everywhere. It hides in plain sight on your lawn, among the dandelions, or in roadside ditches, next to the nettles, but although nearly everyone can spot dandelions and nettles, most of us couldn't identify the broadleaf plantain to save our lives.

I also learned that our grandparents and the generations before them had known better. *Plantago* has been valued for its alimentary and medicinal properties since ancient times. The tenth century Anglo-Saxon medical book called *Lacnunga*, preserved in the British Library, contains an item in Old English known as the 'Nine Herbs Charm' that cites *wegbrade* as a healing herb. Sources from across the centuries claim its pounded leaves as a disinfectant and coagulant, effective in treating deep puncture wounds, such as those received in battle, as well as everyday abrasions. Tea made from its leaves aids the respiratory system as a decongestant and expectorant, while the digestive tract benefits from its mucilaginous properties. As many modern herb catalogues attest, it is still considered one of the best and gentlest remedies for indigestion and constipation. Since all parts of the plant (and those of its equally common sibling, *Plantago lanceolata*, the narrow-leaf plantain) are edible, it has always been valued by the poor and by travellers, pilgrims among them.

All this helps to clarify why it was called 'waybread' (though it has many other names), since such a plant, growing all year round at the edges of tracks from Lapland to the Mediterranean, would have been a boon to people on the move. The leaves, rich in minerals, were eaten raw as salad when young, and cooked, like greens, when older (on learning this, I chopped and boiled some and added it to an omelette: the result was rather like kale). Its seeds and roots were roasted, ground, and added to flour. If it was appreciated as food and medicine, it also had practical value, since its larger leaves could be slipped into footwear as protective cushioning, or used to relieve the pain of blisters. All in all, for much of human history, 'waybread' has been a star – as J.R.R. Tolkein, scholar of Early English that he was, knew well when he borrowed its name for the Elves' sustaining bread in *The Lord of the Rings*. It is we who have forgotten its virtues.

The train of thought set off by my discovery of waybread led directly to the idea for this book. Like the plant, these writings were before me in plain sight. It just took me a while to realise that they might be of use right now, at a time when competing aims are, quite rightly, giving rise to debate. I hope they will be of interest for their collective expression of the Camino spirit, but also for their subjects and the recollections they present, many of which to my knowledge have not been written about elsewhere (at least not in English).

All in all, they are a miscellaneous collection. They date from the mid-1990s to the end of the pandemic. Some are the fruits of research, others draw upon oral history or personal experience. Some were written for the printed page, others to be read as conference papers or given as less formal talks. Several were written for Spanish audiences and translated to appear here, while one was written in English and later presented and published in Spanish. Apart from the odd explanatory note, marked clearly by an asterisk (*), there has been no attempt to 'bring them up to date', nor are they in any particular order. Inevitably, given the time-frame and the course my involvement with the Camino has taken, some topics appear more than once, but far from seeing this as a defect, I think it serves to highlight their importance.

What these writings have in common, however, is that they are grounded in a view of the pilgrimage journey and the experience of traditional hospitality as inwardly transformative. That, to me, is the essential meaning and value of the Camino, notwithstanding all the economic benefits that it has produced in recent years. That experience, as an intrinsic part of the pilgrimage, changes lives for the better, in ways that the times we are living through so desperately need. Keeping this precious experience a viable, universally accessible option matters deeply. So does ensuring that in the rush to claim credit for the pilgrimage as an international touristic phenomenon, its long history as a popular one and the well-documented formative stages of its revival are not selectively air-brushed out of existence.

The danger of forgetfulness can only be resisted by providing a counterweight to it, not just in the material form of albergues where the condition of being a pilgrim is still all that matters, but by defending what those albergues represent, whenever opportunities arise. If anything in these pages can contribute to this 'onward journey', then tenacious little Waybread's name will not have been taken in vain.

La Laguna de Tablas
2 February, 2022

The author, June 2021.
No pilgrims yet, in a bar that is usually full of them:
the Hotel O Cebreiro, still run by the López-Valiña family.

I

The Camino, Then and Now. A Talk Given to the Canadian Company of Pilgrims, Toronto, 30 November 2018

It's wonderful to be with you this afternoon, back in my home city, and in a restaurant called 'El Camino', no less.

Before I talk about what the Camino de Santiago was like 30-odd years ago, I should say a little about its 20th century revival, up to the point when it became walkable at all. I could spend hours on that alone, but I'll begin in the 1940s with *Las Peregrinaciones a Santiago de Compostela,* an immense, three volume work on the history of the pilgrimages to Santiago, written by Spanish historians Luis Vázquez de Parga, José Maria Lacarra and Juan Uría Ríu. Unfortunately, it has never been translated into English – so there is a project for someone looking for a way to spend the next ten years.

Those three volumes brought together everything that had been published up to 1948, and gave chapter and verse on where to find the primary sources. In Paris, the books inspired a group of medievalists at the French National Archives. One of them was René, the Marquis de La Coste-Messalière, who helped to found 'Les Amis du Chemin de Saint Jacques', the first organisation dedicated to the study of the pilgrimage routes, in 1950. Independently, Father Henri Branthomme and two friends had made the pilgrimage on horseback in 1949, filming their journey. This documentary was shown on French television in 1951, and sparked further interest.

On the other side of the Pyrenees, Spanish enthusiasts also devoured those three volumes. One was Francisco Beruete Calleja, an official at the town hall of Estella in Navarre. He and a small group of enthusiasts were already organising cultural events centred on the Camino during the 1950s, and eventually formed the first Spanish association of 'Amigos del Camino de Santiago' in 1962.

Another enthusiast was a young seminarian in the Galician city of Lugo named Elias Valiña Sampedro. He was ordained in 1957, and in 1959 was sent to the isolated and poverty-stricken mountain village of O Cebreiro. There he set about restoring the village, and in so doing, turned it into one of the most important archaeological sites in the country. But more significantly, he wrote a doctoral thesis on the evolution of the legal framework governing the Camino, and began the scholarly and practical task of reviving the historic pilgrimage route he'd studied in all those primary sources identified by Vázquez de Parga and his team.

In 1971 Valiña wrote a simple, pocket-sized guidebook called *Caminos a Compostela* for the pilgrims he was convinced would come. In 1982, he waymarked the road with the yellow arrows that today identify all the Caminos to Santiago. Through the people he met and inspired while studying and walking the route and painting arrows, he created a little chain of associations of 'Amigos del Camino.' In 1985 he began typing out a few pages of notes and news – his famous *Boletin* – to keep everyone in touch. By then, as he had hoped, pilgrims had begun to materialise. In the spring of 1986, I was one of them.

It's hard to accept that 32 years have passed since then. In the history of the pilgrimage to Santiago, those 32 years are just a blip, but more change has taken place in them than in the previous eleven centuries. In 1986, for instance, there was only one 'Camino.' The network of historic roads followed by medieval pilgrims from ports along the Bay of Biscay, the Mediterranean and the south coast still existed, but had fallen into oblivion. The one that counted – *de facto* the only one – was the Camino running across the interior of northern Spain, linking it, via the two Pyrenean passes of Roncesvalles and the Somport, to the four traditional routes across France. Feeding into the starting points of these, in Paris, Le Puy, Vézelay and Arles, was a network of routes extending all over the Continent. Only with the reopening of eastern Europe after 1989 did we discover just how extensive and far-reaching that network was.

Some 1,900 pilgrims, mainly Spanish, received the compostela in 1986. I was one of the few foreigners. After five weeks on the road from Chartres, I crossed paths with a Dutch pilgrim in St. Jean Pied de Port. I was halfway across Spain before I met the next two, both Spanish, in Castrojeríz. They claimed not to have met any other pilgrims, either.

Given today's numbers, this seems incredible. To illustrate: when I spent my first autumn and winter in O Cebreiro in 1989,

I counted five pilgrims between the feast of El Pilar on 12 October and Christmas Day. Today, at any given moment on an average day in O Cebreiro, I can count fifty pilgrims from where I'm standing – and double that number in July and August.

Another significant difference between then and now was that there were comparatively few places on the Camino where one could stay, buy food, and find water.

There were very few parish or municipal 'refugios,' as they were called. A pilgrim had to be prepared for some long stretches – the worst was a 38-kilometre trek across the meseta between Carrion de los Condes and Sahagun on one day, followed by a 39-kilometre one from Sahagun to Mansilla de las Mulas on the next. Pilgrims kept going, because there was no alternative. They had to carry enough food and water to last the distance, since there were days together when none of the places they passed through had anywhere to buy anything. The mountains of Leon were so notoriously depopulated that many pilgrims simply took the train or bus from Astorga to Ponferrada.

That said, when I did meet local people, they were invariably kind and hospitable, offering water, fruit from their trees, even a rest in the shade. I spent a night as the guest of someone who'd seen my photograph in the newspaper, another on an elderly lady's sofa, and another on a pile of rugs in a parish hall. People waved from cars and tractors, they straightened up in the fields to raise a hand, they tooted friendly horns from big trucks, and stopped me in the villages to chat. Walking alone was an ice-breaker, but only of the most positive kind. So often, someone would call after me 'un abrazo al Apostol!' – 'give the Apostle a hug!': the request to be remembered when I finally reached my destination. A pilgrim's journey inevitably became a journey shared.

Most pilgrims return home completely captivated by the Camino: I certainly did. What was it, what is it, that proves so captivating? For me, it has a lot to do with the values that I encountered on the Camino: simplicity, openness, hospitality, respect. I met people committed to reviving and promoting the Camino: Don Elias Valiña, the Marquis de La Coste-Messelière, Don José Maria Alonso, Madame Debril, Pablo ('el Mesonero') Payo, Don Javier Navarro, Don José Maria Mariscal, Francisco Berguete, and a host of nameless but not forgotten ordinary folk. In *A Hug For The Apostle* I called the cumulative effect of meeting these people and the values they represented, in a context of outstanding natural beauty and a lot of exercise, 'the restoration of "right relation" between myself and the world.' I gained a sense of physical, mental and spiritual well-being, a new-found confidence and sense of proportion, a feeling of positivity and goodwill.

When I came home, it seemed important to help make the Camino better known, to support those already engaged in that task. A handful of tiny Camino-related associations already existed in major European countries – not just in France and Spain, but in Italy, the United Kingdom, Germany, Belgium and Holland – so I was clearly not alone. In London I joined the Confraternity of Saint James, a group founded by six British pilgrims in 1983. At the first annual general meeting I attended, in January 1987, I was astonished to find nearly 200 enthusiasts gathered under the same roof.

The conference in Cologne, Germany, mentioned at the end of *A Hug For The Apostle*, took place a few weeks later.

Six months on from Cologne, in September 1987, a conference in Jaca in the Spanish Pyrenees brought together all those fledgling pilgrim associations. This modest gathering would initiate many of the fundamental features of today's 'Camino experience': the credencial, or pilgrim passport; the chain of pilgrim refugios, now usually called albergues, offering simple, donation-based accommodation along the route; the yellow arrow as uniform waymarking; and – at least for Spanish speakers – *Peregrino* magazine, the successor to Don Elias Valiña's mimeographed *Boletín*.

A month after Jaca, the Council of Europe declared the Camino the first 'European Cultural Itinerary', in recognition of its role in forging a European identity. (The German author Johann Wolfgang von Goethe is often quoted as writing that 'Europe was made on the pilgrim route to Compostela,' but I've never seen a reference to a source.) This set off a tremendous wave of study and practical endeavour. The 1990s saw dozens of pilgrimage-related conferences, exhibitions and courses spring up all over Europe each year, but especially in Spain. Camino-related books, from scholarly tomes to personal narratives, poured forth in every European language. Associations of returned pilgrims were founded in Norway and Denmark, Switzerland, the United States, Canada, Australia and South Africa. The opening-up of Eastern Europe brought revelations of the surviving physical evidence of the historic pilgrimage in former Eastern bloc countries such as Poland. Pilgrim associations soon formed there, too.

Goethe's maxim, set into street paving in various languages, Santiago de Compostela. photo Patti Pie Silva

The word 'Camino,' generally used to refer to the main route westward from the Pyrenees, at that point gave way to the designation 'Camino Francés' as the so-called 'secondary routes' in Spain were also resurrected, waymarked and provided with guidebooks. Pilgrims who had walked the Camino Francés and wanted to try something different soon had a range of choices, from the Camino Portuguese to the Camino Primitivo, the Camino Inglés, the Camino del Norte with its many variants, and the Camino Mozarabe, or 'Via de la Plata'. Today, there are eight major, historically documented 'Caminos' that cross Spain to converge on Santiago de Compostela. There are also many local variants, some of them, like the 'Camino del Invierno' invented by politicians to attract pilgrim traffic and boost the economies of the towns along it.

Above all, there was an upsurge in the sense that pilgrims should 'give something back' to the Camino and to fellow-pilgrims: the same impulse that led medieval pilgrims to found 'confraternities' to assist others wishing to make the journey. In our day, it found expression in some notable personal initiatives. In the summer of 1990, a teacher from Cataluña called Lourdes Lluch rented a house in Hornillos del Camino, a village without any pilgrim accommodation, and began welcoming pilgrims into her home. Her example was the genesis of the *Hospitaleros Voluntarios*, an organisation that was soon providing training and administering pilgrim hostels on all the Spanish routes, and continues to do so. In France, two couples were moved to do something similar: they returned home from their Camino, resigned their teaching positions, sold all they had and moved to Estaing in Provence. The Bishop of Rodez offered them a house in which to

Pilgrims waiting outside Refugio Gaucelmo

offer hospitality to pilgrims on the Le Puy route as the *Hospitalité Saint Jacques.* The Belgian association *Oikoten,* and the German *Christophorus Jugendwerk*, began accompanying young offenders along the Camino as part of their aim of social reinsertion.

Then there were Camino projects begun by the pilgrim associations of one country or another. The one all of us know best is Refugio Gaucelmo. I was one of three members of the Confraternity of Saint James sent to Rabanal del Camino in 1989 to see the ruined building we'd agreed to restore. In two years we raised £50,000, and with most of the building work completed, it opened its doors in 1991. As I speak, twenty-seven years later, more than 160,000 pilgrims from

140 countries have stayed at Refugio Gaucelmo, attended by trained volunteer wardens from 16 countries besides the U.K. The albergue offers pilgrims not just a warm welcome, a tranquil garden setting and a restorative night's sleep, but the sense of being in their own home – afternoon tea, facilities for cooking and washing, and breakfast before they set off the next morning. We believe this is the essence of traditional Camino hospitality. It continues to operate, as it always has, through donations from pilgrims, CSJ members, and associations like your own.

The CSJ was not alone in restoring an albergue. The Italian *Confraternità di San Giacomo* created one in the monastic ruins at San Nicolas de Puente Fitero. The Swiss set up another, in an old theatre in Belorado. The Dutch established one at Villamayor de Monjardín, and an American evangelical group opened a house of welcome in the Galician village of Ligonde. These, and the chain of albergues set up by the Guipúzcoa association in the Basque country, were only a few of the many that came into being in the 1990s. As the secondary routes revived, so too did the local initiatives, and those carried out with international support.

By this time, having walked to Santiago on behalf of Multiple Sclerosis research in Canada, the U.K. and Spain, I asked myself, "why not re-enact the other great pilgrimages of the medieval world, to Rome and Jerusalem, bringing in the MS societies of all the countries along the way?" That was how, in the summer of 1989, I found myself setting off on another "Pilgrimage for MS," this time from London to Rome. I left on 1 July, and arrived on 29 September. Three years later I made my third "Pilgrimage for MS" from Canterbury to Jerusalem, arriving on

The author, with map and compass, 1986
photo Peter Phillips

Christmas Eve, 1992. After nearly four months on the road I returned to Spain in early January 1993. The Holy Door of the cathedral in Santiago was open for the first time in eleven years. I passed through with tears of gratitude, aware that had I not first made the pilgrimage to Santiago, I would never have walked to Rome or Jerusalem. I climbed up behind the figure of Santiago above the high altar and gave him another enormous hug.

The Holy Year 1993 was widely promoted both inside and outside Spain. The physical renewal of the Camino became a priority for everyone along it, authorities and residents alike. Pilgrim numbers were rising, and the need for more accommodation prompted improvements in even the smallest and poorest places. Sometimes money was found to pay local residents to clean and maintain them.

In Galicia, the Xunta, or regional government, created a chain of new albergues, beginning with the 80-bed one in O Cebreiro. Yellow arrow waymarks were repainted and ancient pilgrim fountains brought back into use. A new concern for pilgrim safety meant devising byways where the Way coincided with highways, to keep hikers and bikers off the verges of busy roads. Sometimes this led to conflicts between those who defended the physical integrity of the historic Caminos and authorities seeking practical solutions. Many parishes began celebrating Mass at a time of day when pilgrims were most likely to attend. Visitors enjoyed the dual benefits of spiritual attention as well as a chance to see inside the Camino's most evocative monuments, which were otherwise often closed. To round off the Holy Year, UNESCO declared the Camino Francès, from the Pyrenees to the cathedral in Santiago, a World Heritage Site.

Some 100,000 pilgrims claimed compostelas in 1993, a ten-fold increase over the 10,000 of the year before. (That figure itself is fairly astounding when set against the fewer than 2000 of only seven years earlier). There were already concerns about whether the Camino could handle these kinds of numbers, and the six years between the Holy Year 1993 and the next one in 1999 provided plenty of reasons. Europe had entered the era of cheap travel and mass tourism. (The founder of Ryanair even joined the Confraternity for a year, in the run-up to establishing flights between London Stansted and Santiago). Pilgrim numbers climbed inexorably, even in ordinary years.

As the annual analysis published in *Peregrino* magazine revealed, the percentage of pilgrims making the journey for reasons other than 'religious' or 'spiritual' was also on the rise. The idea of what constituted the 'spiritual' motive necessary to gain the compostela, the historic proof of pilgrimage, was broadening along with the increase in numbers. The popularity of 'New Age' beliefs among young people was one factor; another was the increase in more secular-minded pilgrims from non-European countries such as the United States, Canada and Australia. There was also the sudden, large-scale presence of pilgrims from specific countries, such as Brazil, prompted by Paolo Coelho's book *The Pilgrimage,* and Japan, thanks to the appearance of an illustrated guide to the Camino in Japanese, and the promotion of the ancient Kumano Kodo pilgrimage routes. The proliferation of 'Caminos' across Spain, not surprisingly, led to the frequent allegation that 'the only' or 'the authentic' Camino was the one a pilgrim walked or cycled from his or her front door. Many pilgrims adopted the idea that 'the end' of the Santiago pilgrimage was less the tomb of the

Apostle than the rocky Atlantic coast at Finisterre, complete with the 'ritual' of burning their clothes on the beach as the sun sank below the horizon.

By 1999, the last Holy Year of the millennium, a shift had taken place. The Spanish Federation of 'Amigos del Camino' and its review *Peregrino* had always emphasized, in the tradition established by Don Elias Valiña and other pioneers, the need to provide simple facilities for pilgrims and the fundamentally austere character of the pilgrimage itself. In the areas traversed by the Caminos, especially the Camino Francés, pilgrims' modest spending could be seen to have made a real difference to local economies. Family-run bars and restaurants, small shops and accommodation had sprung up to meet their needs, providing employment where there was sometimes little else apart from agriculture.

The governments of regions through which the Camino passed soon realised that it was a potential attraction for tourists, as well as pilgrims. Some foresaw the need for more and varied accommodation and began offering grants to restore abandoned buildings. In the countryside, many of these were rebuilt as B&Bs, or rural guesthouses, charging upwards of 30 euros a night. Older pilgrims who could afford them often found these alternatives more restful than the traditional dormitory-based albergues. More often, the grants were used to set up 'private' albergues: small businesses that enabled the owners to make a living from the Camino. Soon, any establishment offering accommodation was also providing fax machines (to facilitate advance bookings), washers and dryers, phone chargers and computers with connections to the internet. The old sense of leaving everyday life behind dissolved in the face of mobile devices that made it easy – for some, all but obligatory! – to keep in touch. Human ingenuity being what it is, niche markets were no sooner identified than they were filled, the best example of this being the alacrity with which taxi drivers began providing rucksack transport between stops for a few euros per bag.

Until the millennium, pilgrims hadn't needed much money to walk or cycle to Santiago. Many of the parish and municipal albergues continued to be 'free' in the sense that they asked only for a voluntary contribution to running costs, but as pilgrims began demanding more, some, inevitably, began to impose a modest fee. In Galicia, the Xunta's chain of albergues soon imposed a charge of 5, then 6 euros. Within a short time there were few stretches of more than ten kilometres on the Camino Francès without accommodation of one sort or another. On the positive side, this made the Camino more inclusive, since families with children, reasonably active retired people, the unfit, and even people with moderate disabilities could undertake the pilgrimage and find beds within a comfortable distance of the previous night's halt.

A less welcome consequence, as numbers continued to rise, was the competition for those beds, and the tendency for pilgrims to set off in the small hours or take public transport to ensure a place. So-called 'massification' worried everyone, particularly since the first decade of the 21st century contained two Holy Years, in 2004 (in which 180,000 pilgrims claimed the compostela) and 2010 (272,000). How could the pilgrimage remain an experience dedicated to reflection, interior awareness and solidarity, when subject to the stresses and competitiveness engendered by mass tourism?

But the genie was out of the bottle. Flush with European Community funds, the Spanish regions set about making the Camino Francès a world-class tourist destination. Vigorous marketing ensured that it was featured at travel fairs in Spain and around the world. The Camino was an "economic motor" (a phrase often used of it by the politicians of Galicia) that generated prosperity: votes do have a place in all this!

What that means is that in the past twenty years the Caminos have become the focus for many kinds of tourism. Today there are companies dedicated to organizing clients' travel from their nearest airport to the Camino and back again, with hotels and transport paid-for in advance and luggage shipped along. Group tours combine walking stretches of the route with buses along the tougher or 'less interesting' sections, and in the evenings, talks or visits to monuments of cultural interest. The traditional pilgrimage (a journey made under one's own motive power and carrying one's own belongings), with all its inherent risks and surprises, is now a choice, and no longer necessarily the norm. How can one not be pleased that the Camino is now more accessible to the elderly and people with physical problems? Yet I admit to finding it disconcerting to watch the vans of companies with names such as 'Camino Facil' and 'Camino Comodo', delivering to hotels the huge rucksacks and bags of people seemingly determined to enact 'easy' and 'comfortable' Caminos. Somehow, they seem to be missing the point.

Not so long ago, pilgrims accepted that a Camino journey was neither 'easy' nor 'comfortable', and that rising to the challenges it posed could bring valuable life-lessons in return – one of them being to learn what one can live without, as well as what is essential. From the use of GPS to 'instant hydration' devices, every year has seen innovations designed to make the Camino less demanding. The understanding that part of what the pilgrimage has to give depends on physical effort, mental resilience, and the acceptance of at least an element of risk, seems to have been lost along the way.

Recalling the Camino I experienced more than thirty years ago, I am moved, most of all, by gratitude: that sense of gift that I tried to convey in *A Hug For The Apostle.* Some of the changes that have taken place since disappoint me, yet I feel I somewhat guilty for being judgmental about them. They are part of a world-wide boom in experience-based travel, and not, in themselves, surprising. The Caminos are not immune to such influences, nor can it be denied that the Camino phenomenon has lifted parts of Spain out of poverty, creating employment and helping to offset depopulation. What I am prepared to criticize, and do, is the promotion of the pilgrimage for political ends, often beyond what the routes and the facilities along them can bear. I used to believe that the values of the Camino I mentioned at the beginning of this talk could survive anything: for the past several years, I have not been so sure. And yet, in its long history, the Camino has seen it all before, from high prices to false waymarking. If we are distressed by what we see, we must find ways to resist it, change it, or go around it.

First, let us remember that the pilgrimage – that deliberately austere journey motivated by the personal search for meaning or resolution or faith – is still there, as it has been for more than a thousand years. If today's pilgrims have to exercise a conscious option in favour of that kind of journey in the face of all the incentives to choose something else, that in itself is a manner of self-giving to which the Camino's answer will also be gift, whether of insight, or unexpected encounter, or physical confidence.

In finding the space for silence and reflection - two essentials which weigh nothing - some pilgrims say that taking one of the 'alternative' Caminos helps, others that travelling out of season does, even though the weather may be bad. What these less promoted routes offer, in addition to their intrinsic historic and monumental interest, are the unexpected, unhurried encounters with local people, whose gracious and hospitable response to pilgrims is still, as it has been over the centuries, so often what ignites the transforming desire to 'pass it on' or 'give something back' that returned pilgrims so often cite as life-changing. This is the shift in perception that so many identify as crucial; the understanding that arrival at one's destination is not an end, but a beginning. Or, as I expressed it in 1987, and humbly do so again, 33 years later, '...the last steps into Santiago are the first steps of another journey'. The pilgrim walks or cycles the Camino, and then, once back in his or her everyday surroundings, tries to live the Camino. The sum total of such efforts is incalculable, but tangible, and constitutes a quiet force for good in these troubled times that any ideological movement or political party might envy.

Buen Camino, Everyone.

2

Elías Valiña Sampedro and the Camino de Santiago: An Appreciation. The Confraternity of Saint James Third Holy Year Lecture, London, 12 November 1999

It is an honour, and a deeply satisfying but humbling experience, to speak to you this evening, in this third and final Confraternity Holy Year Lecture, about Don Elías Valiña Sampedro. To some of us, it hardly seems possible that the tenth anniversary of his death is only a month away, so vivid are our memories of this diminutive man with the gigantic soul who was the scholarly and tireless defender of the Camino de Santiago, the 'friend and brother to all pilgrims', as the words on his grave attest.

To us, and to his many friends in Spain and in the other jacobean associations of Europe, he was – and is – quite literally, unforgettable. Some of you here this evening will never have met him, though if you have used one of his guidebooks to the Camino Francés, you may feel that you have. To others, especially to our newer members, he may be a name and nothing more. The coincidence of his tenth anniversary and this compostellan Holy Year seems a fitting moment to survey his contribution to the modern-day revival of the Camino, and to paint for a new audience a word-portrait of a most remarkable man.

One of the challenging aspects of this is that his life's work and his vocation as a priest were so inseparable. It is impossible to give a purely chronological account of what he did for the Camino, without bringing in the reconstruction of his beloved O Cebreiro, and the priestly dedication that underlay both of these projects and many others. But common sense dictates that I should begin at the beginning, and so perhaps a brief biography, at least up to the point when the Camino de Santiago became such a dominant part of his life, would be in order.

Elías Valiña Sampedro was born on 2 February 1929, not in O Cebreiro, as many people have assumed, but some 40 kilometres away in the hamlet of Lier, near Sarria, in the Galician province of Lugo. He was the fourth of five children. (Some of you who have stayed in O Cebreiro will know his older sister, Amelia, and younger brother, Eladio, as well as Pilar, the daughter of another sister, María) His outstanding intellect was apparent at an early age. He was sent to the school run by the Mercedarian Fathers in Sarria. The Camino, part of which he walked to get to school each day, was a constant element of his childhood.

At twelve, he enrolled in the diocesan Seminary in Lugo. It was on an outing as a sixteen year old seminarian that he first saw O Cebreiro, and felt the strong presentiment that his future was somehow linked with that windswept village on the path worn over the mountains by the centuries-old pilgrimage to Santiago de Compostela. Then, in the mid to late-1940's, came the epic, three-volume study of the pilgrimage by Vázquez de Parga, Lacarra and Uría Ríu, which fanned one adolescent interest among many into an all-devouring flame. He read voraciously, and to the extent that he was able, travelled. We must recall that the Spain, and particularly the Galicia, of the 1950's was still materially very poor compared to the rest of Europe, and money did not go far abroad. When Elías spent a summer in Paris studying French, he lived in one shabby room and survived on fruit picked up at the end of the day when the street markets closed. Luckily he was naturally austere of temperament, and as many friends will confirm, virtually indifferent to physical comforts, whether food, sleep or possessions.

Following his ordination at the age of 24 in 1953, Elías embarked on a degree in Canon Law at the Jesuit University of Comillas near Santander. This would ordinarily have set him, by the standards of the time, on the fast track for high ecclesiastical office, but this was not then – or ever – to be his destiny. When he finished the degree, he spent some months in Buenos Aires where he had family. On his return, he was appointed priest of O Cebreiro – reputedly after three other priests had turned it down because of its lonely situation and endless winters. From his arrival there in 1959 until his death thirty years later, he would refuse many more comfortable livings to remain in what he came to call *'el Alma de Galicia'* – the soul of Galicia. It was there that a famous eucharistic miracle had occurred in the 14th century, the *Santo Milagro* that gave its name to the romanesque chalice and paten still kept in the church. The same church also housed an image of the Virgin said to have inclined her head at the sight of the miracle,

One of O Cebreiro's pallozas in the 1960s, thatched with bundles of rye stalks secured by a network of braided broom or gorse, all held in place by forked sticks.

and which was, and is, the subject of great devotion in this part of the *alta montaña.**

These features gave O Cebreiro, sited at the top of an arduous ascent on the former Roman road into Galicia, a unique place in the history of the pilgrimage to Santiago. Some authorities date the foundation of the original church to 836, a bare 20 years after the supposed discovery of the tomb of St James itself, and after a great deal of study, Elías came to support this view. But for him, as he often said in later years when he was asked, "O Cebreiro is a place of faith, of simple pilgrimage, in which our sacrifice and penance are readily accepted. The faith of the peasant of the Holy Miracle has been infinitely multiplied.'

Which came first: Elías's fascination with the Camino de Santiago, which led him to one particular historic halt on it, or an unshakable identification with O Cebreiro, which gave him a unique vantage point on the millenarian route that passed through it, westward to the tomb of the Apostle, and back some 700 kilometres to the border with France and the rest of Europe? He could never separate the two. In terms of immediacy, O Cebreiro and the villages around it had the prior claim on his pastoral attention, but for Elías the Camino was always, first and foremost, a Way sanctified by a thousand years of pilgrim faith, a road that ultimately led, by way of the tomb of Saint James the Great, to a greater love of God. His day-to-day ministry was to O Cebreiro and the scattered villages of this mountainous area, or *comarca,* that bore the same name, and to the pilgrims – in those days, only a handful in any given year – who toiled up the gruelling incline from the valley below. But beyond, above and alongside the pressing day-to-day concerns that faced him in these early years in the parish, there was always the vision of the Camino as a once-mighty highway, down which 100,000 pilgrims a year had poured in the 12th century. It linked Spain and Galicia with the farthest reaches of the European Continent – and he longed to see it once again alive with pilgrims of every nation and condition

What did Elías Valiña find when, as newly appointed parish priest in that autumn of 1959, he took possession of the 10th century church of Santa María La Real, one of the most venerable monuments on the Camino de Santiago? What he found would have made a lesser heart sink, a lesser mind reel. The nave lay open to the elements, the roof fallen in, the stairs to the belfry unusable, the floor awash with every rainfall, the plaster dropping from the walls with creeping damp, the chalice and paten of the Holy Miracle preserved from theft only by the infrequency of passers-by. (A friend from Santiago recently told me of visiting the church as a girl of 15 in the winter of 1957, two years before Elías arrived, and encountering a heap of snow in the nave that was taller than she was). The state of the church reflected decades of neglect, for no repairs had been undertaken since before the Civil War.

Just as daunting was the condition of the former monastery, linked to the church by a passageway whose roof had long since disappeared. What is today the dining room and kitchen of the Hospederia was then given over to mules and cows. In the absence of any other source of heat, Elías's predecessors had wisely chosen to inhabit a semblance of a room immediately above, reached by means of a rickety staircase and careful negotiation of the rotting floorboards. In places the metre-thick walls admitted the light of day, the rain and the unceasing mountain wind. The chimney and the roof housed colonies of bats, and a vast manure-pile would eventually take three men a week to disperse.

Even this was only part of the panorama. Enclosing the complex formed by the church, the former monastery and its abandoned garden, was a wall in a state of semi-collapse. Beyond this, then as now, lay the dwellings, each occupied by a family, that comprised the village. These were no ordinary dwellings, but the oval granite-and-thatch *pallozas*, or Celtic survivals, for which O Cebreiro

A PHOTOGRAPH SAID TO DATE FROM 1902 SHOWS A MARKET-DAY IN O CEBREIRO.

has acquired a certain fame among anthropologists. While these fascinating buildings had provided centuries of weatherproof shelter in an inhospitable climate, in the 1950's the people that inhabited them lived, according to their own testimony, in a state of poverty so abject as to be almost inconceivable forty years later. The *pallozas* had earth floors, and housed livestock in one half, people in the other, with smoke from the hearths escaping through the open doors. Apart from bread and the products of the annual *matanza*, or hog slaughtering, the diet consisted of root vegetables grown on the small plots owned by each family – the age-old minifundia system of land tenure still prevailed in Galicia – and the plots were tilled using implements that had not altered since the Middle Ages. Clothing and bedding were made from linen, also cultivated, or from wool, carded, spun, and woven or knitted. Most of the adults could neither read nor write. In the entire village there was no electricity, no running water – or indeed, any source of water nearer than a spring at Liñares, three kilometres away. There was no telephone or other means of communication, nor medical attention other than a doctor based in Pedrafita, who made his rounds on horseback. In winter, which at an altitude of nearly 1300 metres can be both long and cruel, it was common to be snowed-in for weeks; the burial of anyone who died in this season had to wait until spring. And people did die, of cold, of epidemic diseases such as typhus and diphtheria, and of just plain starvation. I have been told, by more than one reliable source, of children reduced to such extremes of hunger that they ate grass.

Some of you may feel that I have dwelt over-long on the state of O Cebreiro prior to 1959, but I confess to having done so for a reason, and that is to show, by contrast with what came after, the scope of what Elías Valiña accomplished in his first half-dozen years there. What, or whom, did he have to work with? The families living in those *pallozas* and a dozen more hamlets, clannish and initially suspicious? Fellow-seminarians, university friends, members of his own family? The answer, within a very short time, would be 'all of these', together with such interest as he could awaken in officials of the regional administration in Lugo, the Xunta in Santiago, various ministries in Madrid, and anyone else he thought could help lift O Cebreiro out of its dereliction.

BETWEEN 1962 AND 1966, THE ANCIENT MONASTERY OF O CEBREIRO WAS RESTORED TO CREATE THE HOSPEDERIA SAN GIRALDO DE AURILLAC

It took three years of letters and visits to persuade the Dirección General de Arquitectura in Madrid to restore O Cebreiro. This was to include the *pallozas,* and the offer of a house to each of the families living in them. During that time Elías sought sources of materials and expert local workmen, and enlisted unemployed men from the area for them to train. He too learned some of the skills that would be needed, such as stone-walling, and began to plant native trees wherever it seemed they might survive. Up to now there had been only one tree in this desolate spot – the rowan in front of the church, which is still there today.

The locals watched, guardedly at first, as he set about all this. He was laying not only the foundations of the work to be done, but of the mutual regard that would spring up between him and almost all his parishioners. What had become a passion for the place included them, and he sought their well-being with equal intensity. He gained their trust through the breadth of his disinterested kindness. He sent a promising youngster to the seminary at his own expense, bought an old woman a set of dentures, and after much wrangling with the powers that be, procured a small pension for O Cebreiro's sole incorrigible alcoholic on the grounds that he was – *an incorrigible alcoholic*. The eve of the Epiphany feast of *Los Reyes Magos* always found him hard at work in the freezing sacristy, not on his homily for the following day, but in making up a bag of sweets for every child in the parish.

In 1962 the work of reconstruction commenced. Archaeologists soon discovered the existence of an earlier, pre-romanesque church beneath the foundations of the existing one. The findings were widely publicised and helped generate further interest in O Cebreiro. Then houses were built and furnished for the village families. Wells were sunk and drains installed to provide running water and sanitation. Electricity and telephone lines were extended from Pedrafita. Once the villagers had abandoned the *pallozas*, the latter were rethatched and taken over by the national Departamento de Belles Artes, one becoming a small museum of rural life that can still be visited. During all this, to save time and transport in O Cebreiro's frequent bad weather, Elías and some of the workmen slept under tarpaulins in the upper floor of the derelict monastery. Elías's elder sister Amelia was persuaded to cook for the crews working on the project, and the

Amelia Valiña Sampedro (left) and Pilar Armesto Valiña with Dr. William Melczer of the University of Syracuse, New York, who regularly brought groups of American students to O Cebreiro during the 1980s

Amidst all the hard work there were lighter moments: here, Elias (left) celebrates the birthday of fellow priest and university friend Manuel Espiña Gamallo.

stories about this, at least until water and light were available, merit a lecture in themselves.

The final stage of all this restoration turned the former monastery into what we know today as the Hospedería San Giraldo de Aurillac. It was named for the 9th century saint and count of Aurillac in France, who had founded a reformed Benedictine community in that town. From there a small group of monks had been sent in 1072 at the request of Galicia's king Alfonso VI to minister to pilgrims passing through O Cebreiro. The Hospedería opened in 1966. It had eight rooms and a spacious dining room, with a wonderful ingle-nook built by Elías himself, which I would venture to say has probably absorbed more fascinating conversations than any other spot on the entire Camino de Santiago. Amelia took on the kitchen, and there began the reputation for solid home cooking that the Hospederia has enjoyed ever since.

Elías saw all this merely as the recommencement, after a long gap, of the building's original function of providing hospitality and spiritual care to pilgrims. Over the 20-odd years that followed, it became clear that this was not just theory, and that his aim far exceeded that of providing pilgrims with a bed and a meal virtually at cost. These simple comforts were welcome after the long day's trek from Villafranca, but they were only part of the formula. To get a flavour of the rest, I would like to quote one of the many later impressions penned on the subject. It is by Don Antonio Viñayo, the abbot of the monastery of San Isidoro in León, writing now of the early 1980's:

> *We have seen Elías surrounded by pilgrims - they were his family – by the fireside on those chill days of fog and sleet, or chatting amicably with them in the plaza in the long summer evenings. He used to prepare the soup in the kitchen, or do the washing-up. An unforgettable image was that of his slight figure appearing in the doorway of the Hospedería at mealtimes, and how he would clap his hands together sharply a few times and shout "Pilgrims! Pilgrims! Time for soup!" Unforgettable, too, the sight of him crossing the plaza with a mug of camomile tea in his hand, heading for the refugio to attend to someone who was ill.*

The *refugio* referred to here was the largest of the now empty *pallozas*, filled with straw as summer overflow accommodation. On chilly nights until the late 1980's pilgrims were often invited to doss down on the floor of the Hospedería's dining room, warmed by the blazing fire. There was always a welcome and meal for those, either pilgrims or local folk, who had no money, just as the Hospedería routinely dealt with blisters, sprains and tendonitis out of the resident medicine chest. While Elías was usually busy with pastoral matters during the day, he made a point of spending time in the dining room and *refugio* in the evenings, eager to hear about the pilgrims' journeys, the lives they had come from and would return to. Their experience, particularly the experience they had of O Cebreiro, mattered deeply to him. Wherever they came from, the aim of what he tried to create was the transcendence of mere nationality, a sense of fraternity that sowed the seeds for service to fellow-pilgrims on the journey, to neighbour and community on the return home. It was as though, as one friend put it years ago, 'what was preached in the church was lived in the Hospedería'.

But apart from that undeniable fact, why has so much attention been centred on O Cebreiro? For the simple reason that it became not just a beloved home and the place above all others where Elías's vocation was to be exercised, but the 'headquarters' for the one-man campaign he waged to revive the Camino de Santiago. It was the setting in which he wrote nearly all his scholarly work. It is to his scholarly work, particularly that relating to the Camino, that I will now turn.

It is almost unbelievable, to me at any rate, that at the same time that the restoration of O Cebreiro was being undertaken and the people of 14 scattered villages attended-to, Elías was also writing a doctoral thesis for the Pontifical University of Salamanca. This was his ground-breaking legal-historical study of the Camino de Santiago, which won national honours in gaining the *Antonio de Nebrija* Prize in 1967. It was subsequently published by the highest academic authority in Spain, the *Consejo Superior de Investigaciones Cientificas*, in 1971. Two articles that appeared at about the same time in the scholarly journal *Compostellanum*, one on the Camino in the valley of the Valcarce and one on the Camino in Galicia, were derived from the thesis. But it was the painstaking research for the thesis, both in archives and on the ground, that underpinned the first of Elías's guides to the Camino, written especially for pilgrims. This was the deceptively simple *Caminos a Compostela*, published on the press belonging to the *Faro de Vigo* newspaper at Elías's own expense in 1971. It was the distillation of a great deal of information into the pocket-sized book he felt pilgrims needed, but no-one knew better than he how much more there was to say. It was, as he put it, 'what was possible at the time'.

The 1970's saw the production of four enormous commissioned works: *El inventorio artístico de Lugo y su provincia,* the first volume of the *Synodicum Hispanicum*, which was dedicated to Galicia, the *Inventorio arquitectónico de interés histórico-artístico de la provincia de Lugo,* and the more than 900 pages of the *Catálogo de archivos parroquiales. Diócesis de Lugo.* Any one of these would be awe-inspiring enough, especially when one considers the countless visits to

Elias on the Camino during the
'Itinerant Study Week' of July 1986

archives, the hours spent sifting through parish records in unheated churches, the treks across country when the snow was too deep to approach a village, and the battered portable typewriter on which all of these works were produced.

There is also the fact that Elías, while engaged on such projects, continued to hoard the hours and days that would allow him to travel some stretch of the Camino. He explored all the byways around O Cebreiro and all the secondary routes in the four provinces of Galicia, but his main preoccupation was the recovery of the Camino Francés. I quote Don Antonio Viñayo again:

> *Elías sallied forth from the heights of Cebreiro to repair the Camino, and not just a short stretch, but rather the whole extent of it in Spain, from Ibañeta and Somport to Monte del Gozo and the streets of Compostela. First he studied the sources in parchments and bundles. Then he walked it, step by step, carefully annotating the out-of-the-way spots, spying out the track through the scrub, identifying ancient hospitals, complaining at times that industrial expansion and ignorance might irreparably destroy sections of the age-old route. And he didn't walk the Camino only once. How many times he did it I can't say, but without exaggerating, I believe it can be estimated at the same number, at least, as the thirty years of his residence in O Cebreiro, and I know he sometimes did it more than once in a given year.*

Don Antonio goes on to ask himself, as everyone who knew Elías did sooner or later, 'when did he ever sleep?'.

These were the years when, having determined the course of the historic Camino, Elías embarked on the waymarking of it, from the

French border to the tomb of the Apostle, with the bright yellow arrows that are still its best-known feature. On at least one occasion in the Pyrenees he aroused the suspicion of the border police, who were convinced that he was marking out a trail for Basque terrorists or smugglers. Similarly, the sight of him streaking yellow paint on the open ground, on rocks and fenceposts and the walls of urban alleyways, often brought the watchful Guardia Civil to a halt. Elías seldom dressed like a priest; and looked still less like one with a yellow paint-pot in hand, but his eager responses always prompted his questioners to let him go. He was quite prepared to talk about the Camino de Santiago as long as they would let him.

In 1980, having by now acquired a reputation as an authority on the Camino, Elías managed to interest the Spanish Secretary of State for Tourism in commissioning a guidebook to the route, to include detailed cartography. It was in seeking collaborators in each of the provinces through which the Camino passed that he sowed seeds for the associations that he saw as necessary if the route, once identified and waymarked, was to be safeguarded. The guidebook, in an inconveniently large format, appeared as *La Guia del Peregrino. El Camino de Santiago* in 1982. Though it credited a team of writers with responsibility for provincial sections of the book, it was in fact Elías who had conceived the idea, planned the work and drawn the maps, done the layout, prepared the text for the press, and carried on relations with the Ministry. The text is basically that of *Caminos a Compostela*, with some amplification in two of the seven sections. It found a ready audience, due to the publicity it received in a compostellan Holy Year, and was reprinted. Two years and several trips along the Camino later, Elías transferred the publication of a revised edition to Editoriales Everest of León. The format was altered to roughly half its original size and the words of the title transposed, though the text and maps remained the same. This version, published in 1985, was the 'big red guidebook' beloved of pilgrims to this day. Elías was dismayed that the publisher would not pay for new maps to be drawn, since he accepted the criticism of the original edition that maps not drawn to scale could be misleading. No sooner was the Everest edition out than he began to plan a completely new guide and cartography which he intended to offer to another publisher, but as we shall see, the time he could devote to this was to be increasingly encroached upon by other Camino-related matters.

By now, as a result of his many journeys and meetings with all manner of people along the Camino, there were many to whom he had transmitted his passion for its defence. On this subject, Elias's natural reticence disappeared and his love of it shone out in a way that was completely disarming. In some places he was able to rouse the last officers of ancient confraternities from their slumbers; in others, it was a question of persuading authorities at every level to be aware of the Camino, to reclaim it and protect it. He haggled with farmers who had planted over it; he begged local *alcaldes* to preserve decaying buildings which he assured them were medieval pilgrim hospitals, he encouraged his fellow priests to welcome pilgrims and provide *refugio*. He wrote hundreds of letters and made equal numbers of visits and telephone calls to people at every level on the social scale. Some considered him a nuisance, but most of those who met him found themselves strangely, if not altogether willingly, captivated

A special number of the 'Boletin', published with a grant from the Diputacion (Regional government) of Lugo. Until then, Elias himself had funded the Boletin and other Camino-reviving activities.

by this small, serious-looking man and his mission. Gradually and not always easily, the nuclei of associations of *Amigos del Camino de Santiago* – in Estella, where there had been a small group since 1962, in La Rioja, Burgos, León, and in his own Galicia - began to expand. When, in May 1985, their first joint meeting, or *Encuentro Jacobeo,* was held in Santiago de Compostela, it was hardly surprising that Elías was unanimously chosen as "Comisario-Coordinador" of the Camino and its fledgling associations.

The mandate Elías received at this pivotal meeting prompted him to launch several new initiatives. The first and most significant was a simple four or eight-page typed newsletter called *Boletín del Camino.* Over the next two years, until it was supplanted by the bigger and glossier *Peregrino*, it kept the associations in touch and steadily increased its circulation. The second venture was an itinerant study week, the *Primera Semana de Estudios Históricos,* along the Galician stretch of the Camino, beginning in O Cebreiro and ending in Santiago. Elías called upon friends who were historians, musicologists, anthropologists and iconographers to give lectures at the traditional pilgrim halts each afternoon and evening, the mornings being reserved for walking the distances between the stops. This novel form of summer school for a time became an annual event.

The third venture was altogether more ambitious. Elías had long been in touch with like-minded scholars in France (where the original *Societé des Amis de Sainte Jacques* had been in existence since 1950) as well as Germany and Italy, and with organisations even farther afield such as our own Confraternity. He and the Spanish associations of *Amigos* were in a position to draw together some of these contacts and to focus on the international nature of the pilgrimage to Compostela. The arrangements for the *First International Conference of Jacobean Associations* that took place at Jaca in Aragón in September 1987 were almost wholly handled by Elías and a small team of local assistants. It is essential to mention that by this time Spain had joined the European Economic Community. The campaign to promote and defend the Camino had suddenly gained considerable force, not only among enthusiasts, but at a provincial and regional level, where it was coming to be seen in political terms as a stimulus to tourism and job creation. In the spring of 1987, for instance, the five Autonomous Regions that together covered the Camino Frances signed a joint declaration agreeing to work together for its recuperation and revitalization. They agreed, among other things, to recover lost sections of the route, to improve access to it, to restore its significant monuments to their glory and lesser buildings for use as *refugios*, to waymark the route adequately and uniformly, to mount cultural programmes relating to it, and so on. This might appear to have realised Elías's aims in one go, and superficially, of course, it did seem a triumph. But in translating his vision into the language of 'politicos', the document lost the gentle way the *Amigos* spoke and wrote, the motivating ideal of the Way of Saint James as a catalyst of personal and spiritual growth, whose end at the tomb of the Apostle marked a new beginning. The chilly phraseology of the 1987 declaration was an ominous, but perhaps an inevitable, cloud on the horizon.

Far more dangerous for the associations, and far worse for Elías, was the internecine quarrelling that marred some sessions of the Jaca

Conference a few months later. The widening jacobean movement, hitherto united by a common aim, was buffeted by gusts of pride emanating from language differences, geographical advantage and personal ambition. The most disinterested and apolitical of men, Elías was shocked and deeply hurt by the ease with which some of those attending cast aside their founding ideals to pursue narrow interests. Besides some excellent scholarly presentations, much good did emerge from the Jaca Conference, such as agreement on the pilgrim *credencial*, the norms for administering *refugios*, and other basic guidelines. But the occasion proved disillusioning for the man who had done most to bring it about, though I am not going to elaborate here on the matters that caused him such distress.

But these events, together with the adoption of the Camino by the Council of Europe as the First European Cultural Heritage Route in October 1987, persuaded Elías that, for better or worse, there was little more that he could do on an organisational level. From this point on he gently withdrew to work on his new Pilgrim's Guide and cartography, the whole of which he redrew after several forays down the Camino during 1988. One pleasing event of that year was that the ever-supportive Diputación of Lugo, at Elías's suggestion, set up the beautiful stone markers that still direct the pilgrim across the province. He was, by contrast, appalled by the intrusive blue and yellow signs planted along the Camino by the Council of Europe, and by the first tour buses that stopped in O Cebreiro whose occupants were on too tight a schedule to allow for a visit to the church and the chalice of the Holy Miracle. 'They have turned the Camino into a race-course' he said.

There was still, and always, his beloved O Cebreiro, and the growing numbers of pilgrims who passed through it, by this time more than 3,000 a year, for whom he felt such a responsibility to provide the new guidebook. There were the members of his family, especially his sister Amelia and his niece Pilar, who helped him run the Hospedería; there were his parishioners, and his many, many friends. I realise that in a talk devoted to his role in the revival of the Camino I can give little idea of what he meant to them, or of his delightfully dry humour, or of how happy a place O Cebreiro, and particularly the Hospederia, was while he was in it. By some outside this charmed domain, however, he was viewed less kindly. Since he observed politicians to be so eager to use the Camino for their own purposes, he challenged them to take similar responsibility for its defects. In a series of newspaper articles, he urged the provision of decent *refugios*, the cleaning of fountains, the creation of rest-areas and the planting of trees. The Diputación of La Coruña received a tongue-lashing for its indifference to the pilgrim's truly horrid experience once past Lavacolla airport: 'abandoned to risk and confusion at the very gates of the City of the Apostle', as Elías put it.

By now, as 'el cura de O Cebreiro' – 'the priest of O Cebreiro' – and champion of the Camino, Elías had spent thirty years in the *alta montaña*, years in which he had pushed himself unremittingly, mentally and physically. By anyone's else's standards, he had achieved a great deal; by his own, there was still much to do. He optimism had bounced back and he was full of projects: not only the new guidebook with its hand-drawn cartography, but a new academic journal of jacobean studies, a conference on the secondary routes to Compostela, a new refugio in O Cebreiro.... He never counted the cost of all this in energy and effort, seeing only the potential doubling of light that such burning of the candle at both ends could realise. But though the mind and spirit may conceive matters in this way, the body is subject to other laws. Through the dark year 1989, when he had one operation after another, it was mind and spirit that kept him going, ever-hopeful of recovery so that he could see these projects into being. To the stream of visitors who came to see him, he talked only of the Camino, seeking to banish the spectre of illness from their minds and his own.

In the wake of his death, we were all left asking 'How can one honour such a man, whose two overriding passions have borne such abundant fruit?' There have been all kinds of answers to this, which may convey some idea of the esteem in which he was held. Thanks to the Bishop of Lugo, a request to bury Elías in his own church was made to Rome, and without much hesitation, granted. The members of the Commission of Experts on the Camino de Santiago, all of whom were among Elías's earliest contacts outside Spain, pressed the Xunta de Galicia to establish an annual prize in his name, for the organisation or person best realising the ideals of the Camino, and in 1995 this became a reality. The Diputación of Lugo republished Elías's award-winning thesis, and erected a monument to him in O Cebreiro. Dozens of the Spanish and European jacobean associations sent plaques which are now mounted on a plinth in front of the church. People sometimes ask me why the Confraternity has not done this, and the answer is that our homage to Elías stands in a niche in the façade of our beloved

Refugio Gaucelmo in Rabanal, in the form of Santiago Peregrino. Over the last ten years there have been more personal tributes than anyone could count. The feeling among those who knew him is of missing his indomitable character more and more, not less and less, and of remembering his wisdom, sometimes with a sad sense of irony at what he would have made of what has been done to - and in the name of - the Camino in the last ten years. His place in the history of the Camino is unique, as I hope I have shown in what was bound to have been a very inadequate account of his life and work. Perhaps the words engraved on his tombstone best sum up the accomplishment, as well as the self-giving, of this very exceptional man:

VIAE SANCTI JACOBI INSIGNIS RESTAURATOR ET OMNIUM PEREGRINORUM AMICUS ET FRATER

(He was distinguished for renewing the Way of St James, and to every pilgrim he was friend and brother).

Please would you consider any applause a tribute to him, as I shall.

(*) For those not familiar with the story, this prodigy concerned a devout peasant named Juan Santin from the nearby village of Barxamaior, who struggled up the hill in a storm to attend Mass. The celebrant, in Don Elias's words, 'inwardly despised' the man for braving the tempest 'just to see a bit of bread and wine'. At the moment of consecration, the bread on the paten changed to flesh and the wine in the chalice to blood, which bubbled over to stain the altar cloths. As the legend has it, the priest fainted, and the statue of the Virgin on the high altar inclined her head, the better to see the miracle. See also pp. 90-91, 94-5

3

The Place of O Cebreiro in the Pilgrimage to Santiago de Compostela and in Popular Devotion, 836 - 2000. An Address delivered at the IVth Study Day organised by the Fundación del Santo Milagro in O Cebreiro, 7 May 1999.

Before beginning this overview of the history of O Cebreiro, I'd like first to acknowledge my debt to the late Don Elías Valiña Sampedro, who was a friend to so many of us. As we know, his pioneering thesis on the legal and historical evolution of the Camino Francès highlighted the area between the river Valcarce and Triacastela, and focused on the age-old pilgrim halt of O Cebreiro, to which he gave the title of 'the soul of Galicia'. His knowledge of sources gives me the confidence to base much of what I say this afternoon on information provided by him, though of course I acknowledge any errors of interpretation as my own. I would also like to thank the residents of O Cebreiro

The church of Santa Maria la Real,
O Cebreiro, in the mid-1950s

who have patiently answered my questions over the years, and whose recollections of devotional life in years gone by make up the last section of this talk.

O Cebreiro's *pallozas*, which have survived throughout the centuries, are evidence of its Celtic origin. In the shallow bowl between the two peaks of Monte Conavia, a small settlement existed even before the Romans constructed the roads – the Vias XVIII, XIX and XX* – that linked Astorga with the north-western coasts of what became Galicia. For centuries these roads were traversed by people heading westwards to the coastal ports and the former Roman settlements that became today's Lugo, La Coruña and Braga. In the early 9th century news of the discovery of the burial place of the apostle James the Great began to circulate, and this route took on a new importance. The tiny settlement, known as *Mons Febrayr* (or, as the *Codex Calixtinus* would call it, *Mons Februarii*), supposedly for its wintry climate, became an important stopping-place. There travellers, early pilgrims among them, could rest and reprovision. In inclement weather, shelter could be found and energies renewed within those durable dwellings of stone and thatch.

What could be offered soon shifted from simply providing shelter to offering hospitality of a very specific kind. The 17th century Benedictine chronicler Fray Antonio Yepes claimed that by the year 836 there was already a Benedictine meson-hospital in O Cebreiro. The archaeological excavations of the 1960s, which revealed the remains of a primitive pre-romanesque church under the existing one, which all authorities date from the 11th century, led Don Elias to agree with this conclusion. The key date, of course, is 1072, when king Alfonso VI of Galicia and Leon, a great supporter of the Cluniac reform, invited the Benedictine community of Aurillac, in the French region of the Auvergne, to take possession of the church and hospital of O Cebreiro. According to Don Elias, this indicated that O Cebreiro was already a vital spot, since it was given to - not founded by - the monks of Aurillac, who moved there to take charge of it. This also supposes that the earlier church must have been replaced by a larger one, better adapted to the growing number of pilgrims. It is possible, given its similarity to the sculptures found in the area around Aurillac, that the original statue of the Virgin in the church of O Cebreiro was brought from France. Thanks to the favour of Alfonso VI, both the statue and the church acquired the name of *Santa María la Réal.*

This monastic outpost on the Way of St James received lands and privileges from the successive kings of Galicia and Leon. Among these were the hamlet of Pereje (located below, in the valley of the Valcarce), from Doña Urraca, the daughter of Alfonso VI, in 1118. Others included the village of Zanfoga, a few kilometres south-west of O Cebreiro, and some houses in Villafranca del Bierzo, from king Fernando II in 1166. Later, other gifts of lands and rights from this same king allowed the community in O Cebreiro to improve its hospitality to pilgrims. Thanks to the extensive cultivation of linen on some monastic lands a few kilometres away (which supplied the spot with its name, Liñares), we can deduce that the comforts offered to them may have included bedsheets for the sick, and the possibility of effecting repairs to clothing.

By the end of the 12th century, pilgrims were making their way to Santiago in numbers not seen again until the Holy Years of our own era. The hospital in O Cebreiro, like most hospitals of its time, received pilgrims without distinction of social class or nationality, and provided all manner of physical and spiritual care. Christian teaching requires that charity be extended to one's neighbour, but the Benedictine Rule is specific in stating that the stranger should be treated as if he or she were Christ Himself. The pilgrim-guest was thus regarded as a sacred being for two reasons: as the embodiment of brotherhood in Christ, and in recognition of the sacrifices being made to reach the apostle's tomb. Anyone who assisted pilgrims in their endeavour shared in their merit.

If this was the theory, in practice, the number of pilgrims now far exceeded the capacity of a small hospital like that of O Cebreiro.

Three pilgrims in O Cebreiro, late 1960s

Using the means at his disposal, the prior decided to erect another hospital on the lands at Pereje, taking advantage of the milder climate of the Valcarce valley to plant vegetable gardens and orchards. Over time, this must have improved the diet of the two communities, and the meals provided to the pilgrims they served.

By definition, the Church required all Christians to receive the sacraments regularly, but expressed particular concern for those, such as pilgrims, who were far from home and possibly exposed to danger and temptation. The monks of O Cebreiro sought the spiritual welfare of all pilgrims, but made a special effort to care for those who arrived sick or on the point of death: hearing their confessions, administering the last rites, and possibly taking down instructions for the disposal of belongings. Those who died in O Cebreiro were buried in the pilgrim cemetery on the north side of the church, today the parish cemetery. Those who died in the hospital in Pereje were also buried in O Cebreiro, unless they were English or French, in which case they were laid to rest in Herrerias, down in the valley just outside Vega de Valcarce, where those nationalities maintained their own cemeteries. I found it moving to learn that during the archaeological excavations in 1962-4, human remains that were very likely those of pilgrims were found near the church in O Cebreiro. Similarly, the designation of the famous 'Puerta del Perdon', or 'Door of Forgiveness' at the church of Santiago in Villafranca del Bierzo can hardly be accidental, since the ascent to O Cebreiro, especially in winter, could easily exhaust or even provoke the deaths of pilgrims who were sick or elderly.

Unfortunately, the decision to build a hospital in Pereje later involved the prior of O Cebreiro in a famous legal battle with the Cluniac prior of Santa Maria of Villafranca, since Pereje lay within his jurisdiction. The problem was eventually resolved more or less satifactorily for both parties, and Don Elías has left us a detailed explanation of the facts. It is enough to record here his observation that the new demands created by the growth of the pilgrimage, which in this case touched on powerful interests in what was really an international dispute, had to be resolved through diplomacy and the evolution of the legal framework. In this, O Cebreiro would play a key role.

During the 13th and 14th centuries, the hospital of O Cebreiro continued to receive royal concessions that ensured its position as one of the most privileged (but by no means the wealthiest) places on the Camino Francés. In the words of Don Elías:

> *Surviving documents give us a clear and real idea of the extraordinary importance of O Cebreiro as a halt on the Way of St James, in the pilgrimage to Santiago de Compostela. The jacobean pilgrimage was the only reason for its existence. The Benedictines imposed a life of sacrifice and austerity in this mountain región, sometimes all but buried by heavy and prolonged snowstorms, motivated only by the precept of charity towards the pilgrims. This same precept moved the kings to favour, through generous donations, this refuge for pilgrims in its mountain fastness, considering it as their own creation, closely linked to the Crown.*

This was especially the case following the eucharistic miracle that took place in O Cebreiro sometime in the 1320s. Unfortunately this was a tumultuous period in Galicia, and privileges such as exemptions from laws and taxes sometimes gave rise to local resentments. By the middle of the 14th century, by which time news of the miracle had carried the name of O Cebreiro to every corner of Europe, wealthy nobles were systematically pillaging the monastery lands. The 15th century saw a further decline in the fortunes of the community, due to the system of *encomiendas* (or ecclesiastical taxes) which allowed the abbot of Espinareda – then administrator – to appropriate O Cebreiro's rents and possessions. We do not know the effect these events had on the pilgrim hospital, but it is logical to suppose that any decline in the economic life of the community would be equally felt in the services it provided.

What undoubtedly must have affected the reception of pilgrims was the great fire that completely destroyed the hospital of O Cebreiro at some point before 1459, since in that year the newly elected Pope Pius II issued a bull in favour of the devastated spot, which conceded *seven-year indulgences to all confessed penitents who visit the Hospital of the Poor of Santa Maria la Real of Cebreiro...situated in the diocese of Lugo, on the Camino de Santiago, called the French Way, and who contribute to the reparation of the said Hospital....* From this we can conclude that once again, the inhabitants of O Cebreiro would have sheltered and fed the pilgrims, perhaps out of charity, perhaps for payment.

This was the situation when, in 1496, Isabella I of Castile and Ferdinand II of Aragon, the 'Catholic Monarchs', arrived in O Cebreiro as pilgrims on their way to Compostela. The ruinous state of the hospital made a strong impression, but they were above all shocked at the lack of veneration accorded to the relics of the now famous eucharistic miracle. The crystal and silver reliquary they donated to ensure a dignified exposition of the relics can be seen today, on either side of the chalice and paten associated with the miracle. Their most important act, however, was to seek papal intervention to separate O Cebreiro's church and hospital from the French mother house of Aurillac, and incorporate it into the Benedictine congregation of Valladolid, which was soon to spearhead the reform of the Order in Spain.

O Cebreiro received further gifts and privileges during the reign of the Catholic Monarchs. Its buildings were restored, and the generous care of pilgrims recommenced. In the words of Don Elias, O Cebreiro was once again *a guiding light on the jacobean route,* and he assures us that *all pilgrims went on their way contented with the good treatment they received.* Pilgrims were provided with a dry bed, a meal of nourishing soup or other dish with bread and wine, and alms for the next day's march. The story of the eucharistic miracle, spread by guidebooks, poems and pilgrim songs, meant that no-one passed through O Cebreiro without seeing and venerating the holy relics. Travellers also venerated the image of *Santa María la Réal*, popularly known as *La Virgin de O Cebreiro* or *Nuestra Señora de los Remedios* (Our Lady of Healing).

The political and religious turbulence of the 16th century brought about the decline of the pilgrimage from outside Spain. Emperor Charles V (Spain's king Charles I) spent a night in O Cebreiro in 1520, but in the centuries that followed, most references to it come from pilgrim narratives. Domenico Laffi, an Italian pilgrim, and the so-called *Peregrino Curioso* ('Curious Pilgrim') from Spain, both describe in detail the miraculous relics, the generous hospitality provided to pilgrims by the few elderly monks, and the derelict condition of the monastery and hospital, devastated once again by fire in 1641. Other narratives remind us of the severity of the climate and the kindness of the villagers. A Spanish pilgrim, one of a group returning from Santiago in 1642, reported passing through Alto de Poio and O Cebreiro in early March and losing their way in heavy snow. When they reached '*the village of Zebrero, which belongs to the Benedictines, who have a small monastery there...we saw no-one because the village was virtually buried in snow.*' They were saved by a local family that offered refuge in their palloza (of which the pilgrim left a good description) and shared all they had with the unexpected visitors.

From the 18th century until the expropriation of church property in 1835, O Cebreiro shared in the decline of the pilgrimage that was its reason for existence. We know that in 1804 there was enough money coming in to replace the roof of the church with slates for the first time, rather than with the usual thatch. None the less, French troops caused serious damage in 1809, during the Peninsular Wars. The church's record books had been hidden for safekeeping in the home of a parishioner, but on being found by the soldiers, were burned, along with the house itself. Many liturgical objects were stolen, though not the relics of the eucharistic miracle, which were more successfully hidden in the nearby hamlet of Foxos.

The Benedictine community continued to serve the inhabitants of O Cebreiro and the dozen villages situated on the slopes of the surrounding mountains, but there remained only the prior, a handful of monks and a few servants. A note from a visit made by the abbot of Valladolid in 1819 informs us that *the building and hospital of O Cebreiro has been knocked down, and now the pilgrims and other poor folk must resort to the inn, thus becoming the victims of the innkeeper's avarice. The Father Prior has been ordered to begin work on restoring the hospital building, and until then, to ensure that decent accommodation be provided for pilgrims at the inn.* It seems that the monks had contracted the innkeeper to do the work that they themselves were no longer able to undertake, but that he took advantage of his position to fleece the pilgrims.

The year 1835 brought the dissolution of properties owned by the religious orders. The Benedictines hung on for a further twenty years in O Cebreiro, the last two monks departing only in 1858. Their devotion is revealed to have been strong indeed, since they asked the Bishop of Lugo to re-ordain them as diocesan clergy and allow them to return to O Cebreiro. The monastery became a rectory and the church a diocesan Marian shrine, with the two former monks as priests in charge. The church became a place of pilgrimage in its own right, with the image of the *Virgen de los Remedios* taking precedence even over the relics of the *Santo Milagro*. Without its rents and privileges, the church now depended on the donations of visitors to the shrine, and parishioners' tithes.

Thus began a century of neglect, during which, for lack of funds, O Cebreiro's ancient buildings deteriorated almost to the point of no return. We should resist the idea, however, that during that time the spiritual life of the place was as derelict as its buildings. Documentary sources are few, but collective memory affirms that the annual round

THE CHALICE AND PATEN OF THE EUCHARISTIC MIRACLE ON DISPLAY, MID-1950S.

of liturgical feasts, with their vigils and processions, continued, and that story of the Holy Miracle ensured that feast days centred on the eucharist had a particular resonance. Parish records mention *cofradias*, or devotional societies, of the Blessed Sacrament and of Our Lady, at least until 1935. The parish received periodic visits from the Bishop of Lugo, and each year, on the Sunday following the feast of Corpus Christi, it welcomed the diocesan pilgrimage. Other groups based in Lugo – military, medical, educational – and societies dedicated to *adoracion nocturna* or all-night prayer, made excursions to O Cebreiro, as did visitors from the neighbouring diocese of Astorga. Now and then the village was visited by groups from abroad. The English diocese of Westminster made a pilgrimage to Santiago in 1913, and took a detour to visit the site of the eucharistic miracle.

The Camino de Santiago continued to be the only means of access to O Cebreiro until after the Civil War. For visitors who were physically capable, pilgrimage on foot from Vega de Valcarce or Pedrafita do Cebreiro could include the hamlet of Barxamayor, where they could see the house of the peasant Juan Santín, the protagonist of the Holy Miracle, and the tree he is said to have planted. He is buried in the church in O Cebreiro, in one of the niches in the chapel where the chalice and paten are on view. In the other niche is buried the ordained monk who was celebrating Mass on that momentous day when, in an instant, his faith was shown to be insufficient, then rendered complete.

Of the successive parish priests appointed to O Cebreiro after 1858, little more is known than their names, but from 1927 to 1933, the religious life of the village is illuminated by a series of newsletters published by one of them, Don Manuel Cageao, entitled *El Mensajero del Santo Grial de O Cebreiro* ('The Messenger of the Holy Grail of O Cebreiro'). Its editor evidently had a passionate interest in identifying the chalice of the *Santo Milagro* with the grail of the Parsifal legend, and dedicated many pages to this subject. This singular little publication also gives us more immediate information. The editor wrote scathingly about the lack of a decently paved road for vehicles coming up from Pedrafita, citing the difficulties of access for the groups of pilgrims originating in Valdeorras, Mondoñedo, Viveiro, Sarria and Lugo, which had visited the shrine in the summer of 1930. Thanks to the issue of 'The Messenger' of August 1927, we learn of another fire in the church of O Cebreiro, and we can put a date to one of the countless restorations of the statue of the Virgin. Don Manuel wrote that she

O Cebreiro's annual 'fiestas', held on 8 and 9 September, have always attracted huge crowds. Here, the Virgin begins her processional journey around the village.

was *taken to Lugo in 1922 on the orders of his Excellency the Bishop, so that the damage to it occasioned by the fire of the previous year could be repaired...*, and that, *robed in a silk tunic, bearing on her breast a painted image of the Holy Grail... with the Child seated on her left arm...* the Virgin maintained the legendary inclination of her head. A sculptor from Santiago called Magariños was commissioned to re-create the hands of the statue, and a priest called Rodríguez Moscoso, to repaint the face. Another issue, in August 1930, describes the campaign being organised whereby every parishioner was to contribute to a fund to buy a silver crown for the statue.

The most interesting information has to do with the celebration of the famous *fiestas* in September. Referring to a document dating from 1820 signed by all the residents of O Cebreiro, the *Mensajero* affirms that the extension of the patronal feast of 8 September to include the commemoration of the Holy Miracle had its origin in a promise on the part of the parishioners, made in thanksgiving for favours received through the intercession of *Nuestra Señora de los Remedios*. Possibly this was the reason why the celebrations on 9 September were always known as the *Fiestas del Santo Grial* or *del Santo Milagro*, given the importance the day soon came to have. In time, the *fiestas* would come to occupy four days, from the evening of the 7th to the morning of the 10th. This popular pilgrimage, or *romería*, has always attracted thousands of people from Galicia and León, the numbers in the 1930s reaching some 30,000. They became the high point of the year, combining intense devotion with festivity, and marked the transition between the hardworking life of the summer and the satisfaction of the harvest season.

The collective memory of the residents of O Cebreiro has confirmed much of the information supplied by 'The Messenger' and helps us gain an idea of how these festivities were celebrated. Preparations were already underway by August 31st, with the beginning of a novena and the singing of traditional motets. Later, on the eve of the patronal feast, the pilgrims who had come from Lugo on foot would arrive, many of them barefoot, with bleeding feet, after days and nights of walking. To mark the beginning of the festivities, there was *a tremendous round of bell-ringing, the setting-off of large firecrackers and the performance of various musical compositions.* On the 8th, *a famous*

A FORMAL PHOTOGRAPH CELEBRATING THE COMPLETION OF O CEBREIRO'S RESTORATION, 1962-66, THOUGH THE PHOTO MAY DATE FROM SLIGHTLY LATER. DON ELIAS CONTEMPLATES THE SHADOW CAST BY THE SCULPTURE OF CHRIST ABOVE THE NEW ALTAR.

regional quartet strolled through the streets of O Cebreiro, *playing a variety of morning hymns* before the celebration of the first Mass at five in the morning. The number of pilgrims steadily increased as the day wore on, and included some from the nearby villages who covered the distance to O Cebreiro on their knees, as penitents. It was common for some to reach the church all but fainting from such an exertion, and to emerge with strength renewed after appealing in prayer to the Virgin. Masses and confessions were celebrated throughout the day, with solemn processions at noon: on the 8th, with the statue of the Virgin, wearing her long train of blue silk and carried on a palanquin by adolescent girls from the parish, and on the 9th, the Virgin, accompanied by the relics of the *Santo Milagro*. Parishioners followed the procession on its way around the village.

The church was filled with lighted candles, the visible sign of the many petitions being offered. Flowers abounded, and wax images of animals and body parts (suggesting the nature of the problem for which intercession was to be sought), were sold from stalls outside the church. The faithful gave sacks of grain, hams, baskets of grapes and tubs of apples that would later be auctioned by the sacristan in the church porch. As they are during the *fiestas* today, the streets were lined with stalls selling every variety of food and drink, clothing and household utensil. Vermouth was the drink of choice for the young men that gathered around the bars set up in tents. Extended families spread out tablecloths on the hillside at the far end of the village to share the mid-day meal or afternoon 'merienda', serenaded by itinerant musicians – a piper, a drummer and a blind violinist - who turned up every year for the *fiestas*, rain or shine.

The late afternoons offered a notable variety of diversions, not just open-air sports, dances and bagpipe competitions, but also *greased-pole climbing, wrestling, and football games in the Pozo de Area and the Chao de Poza*, concerts, recitations of poetry about the legend of the Holy Grail, a fashion show with 'modesty' as the watchword, and a horse race *from Chao da Cruces to Fonte-Landeira....* Truly, these were occasions to remember, at which family ties were renewed, young people allowed to mingle, bargains struck, and employment found. Music and dancing went on into the night.

Among the events recorded by *El Mensajero* in 1933 was the visit on 14 January of a group from the National Archives that included José Maria Lacarrà and Luis Vázquez de Parga. These two great historians, together with a third colleague, Juan Uria Riu, would soon begin work on their comprehensive account of the jacobean pilgrimage, which first saw the light of day as the winner of a national prize competition in 1945. As such, it was widely publicised – and caught the attention (although we have no written record of this, only his recollection as told to a friend), of a 16 year-old seminarian from Lugo. Later that year, he and his classmates were taken on an excursion to O Cebreiro, where what he had read suddenly took on a life of its own.

The rest, of course, is history. In 1959 - by then ordained and bearing a degree in Canon Law - Don Elias Valiña Sampedro was appointed parish priest of O Cebreiro, accepting gladly what several others had refused. His 30 years here would witness the recuperation and rebirth, not only of this millenarian spot, but of the entire Camino Francés. A restored O Cebreiro once again became famous for its hospitality to pilgrims. Through that hospitality, its name continues to be known around the world, because wherever there are pilgrims, there too will be the memory of O Cebreiro.

(*) *According to the Itinerarium provinciarum Antonini Augusti*, a 3rd century register of the Roman Empire's roads and settlements

4

Gifts And Reflections. An Address given at the Confraternity of Saint James AGM on 25 January 2003 to mark its 20th Anniversary and the Author's farewell as Chair.

I have called this talk *Gifts and Reflections* because that is the title that sprang to mind, quite spontaneously, when Marion* rang me one morning in early December and told me I had precisely half an hour to provide one before the AGM papers went to the printer. But I think – on reflection – that, rather like those attempts at spelling a word when you realise you had it right the first time, *Gifts and Reflections* is as good a summary as any for what I want to say in this, my last presentation as Chair, but I hope not my last before a Confraternity audience.

The difficulty, of course, has been in knowing where to begin – and so I am approaching 'the beginning' in a round-about way, by means of a little imaginative exercise. I invite you to close your eyes and imagine yourselves on your favourite stretch of the Camino Francés: it could be a path through the vine country of Navarra, some Galician mountain track, or even that long, oak-lined stretch of road into Rabanal. It's a cool but sunny day in the month of November. In the distance, there is a group of five pilgrims – or perhaps it would be more accurate to say, 'four plus one', because one of them lags behind, struggling with an immense and weighty rucksack.

As they approach us, we can see that they are very different in age and appearance, and that hand gestures and a lot of laughter are making up for the lack of a common language. I will tell you a little about them. A step or two ahead of the others, like a shepherd leading his flock, comes a Spanish pilgrim (a policeman, as he told me one evening over a glass of wine). His all-weather clothing and the rhythmic swing of his *baston* suggest an experienced walker. Slightly behind him comes a younger man, fit and tanned, but perhaps more at home on the beach in Rio than in keeping a weather eye out for yellow arrows. The diminutive young woman walking next to him hails from Quebec; she set out from Le Puy on her 21st birthday, feeling the need to know what being on her own was like after growing up in a commune. Then comes an impressive figure: a black pilgrim, six feet four inches tall, wearing a long coat that almost sweeps the ground. He emigrated from West Africa to France, and now he is a fisherman in the port of Marseilles. His rucksack seems to weigh nothing at all, and he frequently turns around to check the progress of the fifth pilgrim, a hundred yards to the rear – a Japanese, who even without his burden would not reach the chest of his companion. It would appear that he has brought with him all the utensils of his trade as a chef in Kyoto, on the other side of the world.

Five pilgrims – four men and a woman – from five continents and six countries: Spain, Brazil, Canada, Cameroon via France, and Japan. Their ages range from 21 to 50, and on the face of it, they have nothing in common except the fact of being pilgrims, and of having set out on the Camino alone. Somewhere between Roncesvalles and Estella, each one met up with one or more of the others. By now they give the impression of having known one another all their lives.

Why have I asked you to indulge in this exercise and summon up the persons of these five pilgrims? Very simply, because since I had the good fortune to coincide with them in Estella in November of the year 2000, and to observe them day after day all the way to Galicia, I have thought about them a great deal, always with gratitude, for in a sense they refreshed my own appreciation of the Camino. To me they were five living examples of what we so frequently call 'the spirit of the Camino' – which is no more and no less than fraternal charity. I recall the generous and spontaneous way in which each of them cared for the well-being of the others, and their contagious delight in one another's company that overcame any obstacles of communication. Some beautiful images remain in my mind: the Spanish policeman bandaging the blistered feet of the Japanese, the tall African carrying the chef's heavy rucksack along with his own; the five trying to decide what to buy for the supper they would prepare and eat together in the albergues, with the trilingual Quebecker translating for everyone.

My five pilgrims were aware that they had each received something special through having encountered one another. I asked them what they would do when they reached Santiago. They had given a great deal of thought to this, and the answer was, "walk to Finisterre, each alone, to relive their original experience...and once there, walk back again together, to rediscover the happiness of companionship again, for a few last days before making their separate journeys home". I could hardly bear to think of them saying goodbye, but they seemed more philosophical: there is the internet, after all! I saw them last in O Cebreiro, as I was staying there over Christmas and they were carrying on. Watching them set off down the cobbled street in the rain, I reflected not only on what a gift their meeting had been for each of them, but what a gift my time with them had been for me. They had shown me that the spirit of the Camino was alive and well, and brought the reasons for being involved with it back into sharp focus. Some weeks later, by which time they must all have been back in their own countries, I reached Santiago myself, and found a note from them, left for me on the notice board in the Pilgrim Office. It was signed "Pilgrims, forever", and so perhaps they will be back.

One reason why the example of these pilgrims made such an impact, I think, is because it brought to mind my own first pilgrimage to Santiago, when life itself was less complicated and the Camino less so still. Perhaps walking out of season, as I and my five pilgrims did two years ago, is now the only way to ensure a peaceful pilgrimage. Things were very different in the Confraternity's early days. Fewer than 1000 pilgrims a year made their way to the shrine of Saint James during the early 1980s, nearly all of them along the Camino Francés. Walking in the spring of 1986, I had reached Castrojeríz before I met my first two of them! There were perhaps a quarter of the number of today's refugios in existance then, which made for natural or obligatory 'etapas', some of them exceedingly long. Above all, my daily walk was enriched by very frequent contact with local people, whose spontaneous interest and kindness made a deep impression, and with a dozen or so amazing people scattered along the length of the Camino who had dedicated their lives to assisting pilgrims. In a recent talk at a Federation Conference in Spain, I called this unofficial support network 'the fifth pillar' of the Camino (the other four being local governments, the associations of Amigos, the church and the Hospitaleros Voluntarios). I think it no exagerration to say that generations of local people, living along the Camino and extending hospitality to pilgrims as the natural expression of their faith and their own sociable and generous characters, have played a major part in keeping the pilgrimage alive. This was especially true between the 1830s, when the monastic foundations were despoiled, and the 1980s, when the associations of Amigos came into being and local governments began to view the pilgrimage as a potential source of economic development.

They, again, were 'the spirit of the Camino' in action. They exemplified that spirit to some of us and to countless others, and in doing so aroused in many of us the desire to 'give something back' to the Camino, to serve other pilgrims as we had been served. The Confraternity, only 500 strong when we wrote to the Spanish Federation in the spring of 1988, grew to meet the challenge of rebuilding a ruin to provide a restorative experience for pilgrims on a particularly gruelling stretch of the route. In this we enjoyed the help of many others, especially our friends from the association of Amigos del Camino de El Bierzo, but most of the planning and fundraising came from the Confraternity, in a sustained campaign that drew us closer together in a common endeavour. But has *Refugio Gaucelmo* been our gift to the Camino, or the Camino's to us? As I see it, the soul of the Confraternity was forged in Rabanal, and that in seeking to give, we have, quite unwittingly, brought down upon ourselves a shower of blessings of every kind. In particular, I would mention here, on this celebratory anniversary, the welcome we have always been given by the people of Rabanal, the friendships, the precious contacts with pilgrims, the appreciation shown to us by the bishops of Astorga that we have worked with, and the award of the first *Premio Elias Valiña* in 1996. We have had our momentary difficulties, of course, but that is to be expected in the nature of what we have attempted. The process of learning and improving what we can offer to pilgrims, in collaboration with our friends from El Bierzo and our Benedictine neighbours, has been a positive experience that has enriched our lives, at the same time as it has drawn the best from us. We continue to believe that the warm welcome, the clean and peaceful environment, the sense of being in their own home, create the conditions for pilgrims to gain the most from the companionship of others. We hope they will find, in the beautiful services available in the church a few paces away, a deeper understanding of the love and sacrifice implied by pilgrimage itself. We sometimes smile at hearing *Refugio Gaucelmo* referred to as "the English one", because we know that it is probably the first truly international albergue on the entire Camino, in which wardens from 16 different countries, including England and Spain, have welcomed more than 71,000 pilgrims since 1991.* With surprise and quiet joy, the Confraternity has assumed a modest place, as one stone among the many, as part of the 'fifth pillar'. There can be no greater gift than this, and rather like one definition of happiness - that it steals up on you while you are thinking about something else – that gift has been an unexpected by-product of a great deal of self-giving on the part of many people.

The Camino de Santiago, and with it, the Confraternity, changed very quickly with the promotion of the Holy Year 1993. In retrospect, we can see that even the most problematical changes have contained their element of good. The torrent of publicity that has produced the massification so often complained of by all the 'pillars' - and by pilgrims themselves - has moved many people to walk or cycle to Santiago who would never have done so earlier. It has also helped to swell the Confraternity's membership. Internet sites – the Confraternity's among them – inform and inspire not only a new generation of pilgrims, but pilgrims from backgrounds once untouched by this kind of knowledge. My five pilgrims were cases in point: another thing they had in common was having explored the subject of the pilgrimage on the internet. And where else, if not on the Camino, could five such very different people ever meet, and over a few weeks come to know one another on a basis at once so disinterested and so intimate? (I cannot think of anywhere else, and if any of you can, I would be interested to know what it is.) Similarly, the millions spent on Camino infrastructure – over-abundant and intrusive signing, for instance – is often castigated (and often rightly), yet without the many new albergues that have shortened the distances between stops, the Camino would have remained the preserve of only the strongest walkers and those with unlimited time. Any ideas about 'inclusivity' we may have rest solidly on the provision of facilities during the past ten years. The same may be said about our recommendations to try alternative routes to the Camino Francés. It is only fairly recently that these have become sufficiently viable for us to suggest.

And yet – I would be less than honest if I did not acknowledge that promotion has brought its perturbing aspects. Most of them, I think, derive from altered attitudes and expectations, although the pressure of numbers is responsible for the competitiveness that sets pilgrim alarm clocks to 4 am, to be sure of getting a bed at the next night's stop. I will confess to a flicker of disillusion when – from my frequent vantage point behind the bar in the Hospederia in O Cebreiro – I overhear pilgrims whose 'credenciales' I have just stamped, planning the next day's journey by bus, or grumbling because the refugio or the route did not, in the grumbler's opinion, live up to what the guidebook or the website had promised. One veteran *hospitalera* comments wryly on the same kind of experience: "Before", she writes, "when July 25th fell on a Sunday, there was a Compostellan Holy Year. Now there are "Jacobeos", more terrible than Al Mansur himself". In 1999 there were 'pilgrims' who (and I quote her again) "before saying "buenos dias", ask whether there is a washing machine, dryer, television (they have to see the Cup Match) microwave, internet or fax".

Yet our response to this kind of thing, I think, cannot be one of more than momentary disappointment. The spirit of the Camino continues its transforming magic, turning tourists into pilgrims, as it has done these many centuries. The Confraternity has sought – and will always seek, I hope - to be true to the spirit in which it was conceived. Great increases in numbers, changing attitudes and the demands of external bureaucracy have all been met with a consistant determination to keep the focus of attention where it ought to be: on providing for pilgrims, as individuals, and with as great a degree of personal attention as possible. In a decade we have gone from a compact organisation in which virtually everyone knew everyone else, to one numbering well over 2,000 members, a fair proportion of whom live overseas. We have had to learn and to strive to keep our outreach a personal one (and here I pay unreserved tribute to Marion), making choices that foster contact and involvement, without sacrificing the efficiency needed to fulfil our aims and obligations. We have tried, not just to do good things, but to do them in a good and satisfying way, a way consistent with what it is that we are encouraging other people to do! As a personal observation, looking back over my 17 years on the Main Committee, I can say that the Confraternity enjoys a singular harmony: it has never been beset by cliques or factions, split by feuds or divided into camps. Within its ranks are represented a host of interests, abilities and differences, yet we have always been able to summon forth the unifying principle, the common aim, which has drawn our particular contribution from each of us and our best from all of us. That is 'the spirit of the Camino' at work, and it is a great gift.

Our task, as individual pilgrims who have experienced the Camino, as members of this collective pilgrim body called the Confraternity, and of the wider jacobean community, is to participate, with others who share and treasure that experience, in ensuring that it survives. There are obviously limits, imposed by our geography and by our status as a foreign association, to what we can do regarding the defence of the Caminos as physical entities, unless we are asked by the local Spanish association – as we have been, on several occasions – to bring our influence to bear. The precious human interchanges, of which we all no doubt have our own memories, are perhaps easier to protect, because we can respond to them individually by expressing our gratitude directly. We witness to them individually, by heartfelt 'going and doing likewise' for someone else, somewhere else. That is how we whose lives have been altered by our experience of the Camino transform the world around us, person by person and moment by moment, into a reflection of it.

We all know that the pilgrimage to Santiago does not end there. Rather, as I have written elsewhere, "if the journey meant anything, it meant that the last steps into Santiago were the first steps of another journey". I know, as you do, that this insight comes a good while before we ever reach Santiago. It comes when we have ceased to worry about whether we will manage to cross the meseta, whether the long day between Rabanal and Ponferrada will finish us off, whether the ascent from Vega de Valcarce to the gateway of Galicia will bring on tendinitis or blisters or worse. This insight comes - another unexpected and unlooked-for gift - when we have finally achieved the last of the daunting physical challenges, and we know, because there are no more major obstacles between us and Compostela, that all being well, we are going to make it. It dawns upon us that in less than a week we will be there: we will pass through the Portico de la Gloria, we will offer our prayers of sorrow and thanks and petition, we will give Saint James his hug.... and then, this transforming insight whispers, "we will go home".

A Hug for Saint James at the Cathedral in Santiago de Compostela.

And here, the pilgrim – I, or you – experiences with the eyes of the heart the contrast between the simple and harmonious way of life of the Camino, and the hurry, complication and excess of the lives he or she – or we – left behind, and are going back to. To see that contrast is already to begin the inner, and sometimes painful, process of transformation: that process of re-evaluating and choosing and discarding through which we allow ourselves to be conformed by, and to, the spirit of the Camino. I have long thought that this insight about how we are going to assimilate the pilgrimage into the life we are going back to – or rather, *since we come to understand that we must rephrase the question*, how we are going to transform the life we are going back to into a fair copy of the pilgrimage – comes, like a cool breeze on the cheek, when we pilgrims can finally rest after the gruelling climb up to the tiny but very significant halt of O Cebreiro. This is not, of course, a new insight; I think that Elias Valiña, of whom all of you will have heard, understood O Cebreiro in that way, and of course there are legions of pilgrims who will attest to it, too. And although I cannot prove it, I would be surprised if the importance of O Cebreiro in the spiritual geography of the Camino was not something that was understood a very long time ago. It seems to me that for this reason, O Cebreiro is a truly holy place, quite in addition to the fame of its *Santo Milagro*, for another 'holy miracle' takes place every time a pilgrim understands that he or she can choose to live as one for the rest of their earthly life.

It is in this context that I want to set a reference to yet another gift – lost in the mists of time, and yet as present to us as O Cebreiro is present to us. It was in 836, according to the Benedictine historian Father Antonio Yepes, that members of the Order built a simple church in the hamlet where the Roman road between Astorga and Compostela crossed the mountains that border Galicia. News of the discovery of St James's tomb had been circulating (depending on one's dates) for barely twenty years. There may have been pilgrims, even at this early date, though the first recorded ones would not appear for another century. Still, archaeological evidence is generally agreed to confirm Father Yepes. The Benedictines from Aurillac, who took up residence in O Cebreiro in 1072 at the invitation of king Alfonso VI, were thus taking over an existing monastery, not establishing a new one. They came to attend to the pilgrims by then making their way in large numbers to the shrine of St James. They stayed - a handful of monks, and every now and then a novice from France, or nearer to hand, from Spain - through the centuries when pilgrims passed through in their tens of thousands, and the later ones when there were hardly any, through war, famine, pestilence and the terrible mountain winters, decade after decade, century after century. They sustained pilgrims, and the pilgrimage itself, until the confiscation of Church property of 1835, and even then, the last two monks did not abandon O Cebreiro until 1858. All told, there was a religious community of some kind there, with a specific mission to pilgrims, for more than a thousand years. Is it too obvious to suggest that the hospitality extended to pilgrims by what I have called 'the fifth pillar' owes much to the living example of this community and others like it, that together made it possible for pilgrims to reach Santiago in past centuries?

Considering the priority we all place on hospitality to and for pilgrims, I have found it strange that the Benedictine community based in O Cebreiro seems to have been forgotten. Don Elias, of course, wrote movingly about it in his doctoral thesis, and in 1964 named the restored Hospedería after St. Gerald of Aurillac, but apart from that, historical amnesia reigns. I am trying to make a modest attempt to rectify this, by writing to the Bishop of Lugo, asking to be allowed to commemorate the Benedictines of O Cebreiro with an explanatory bronze plaque, to be placed near the Hospedería. Assuming that he accepts this proposal, the gift you have so kindly collected for me will be put towards it. In the context of the Camino, I see this as a gesture of elementary justice and gratitude, but I also hope it may restore to the people of O Cebreiro an essential part of their own history, and to pilgrims, bring joy to know that they have been cared for in this emblematic spot for more than a thousand years.

With that, I approach the end of this over-long talk. It remains only to thank you, yet again, for your confidence and collaboration during the past eight years. I in turn have every confidence in the future of the Confraternity. It has been a privilege to be able to give back a little of the much that I have received. I am aware of owing it so much – far more, in fact, than I could ever put into words. May St James protect and favour it, and all of you, and all pilgrims, who – from wherever they set out – travel onwards together.

(*) Marion Marples (1950-2019) Secretary of the Confraternity of Saint James for over 25 years

(*) To the end of the 2019 season, 20 countries, and 161,697 pilgrims from 140 countries.

LAURIE NEXT TO THE PLAQUE, UNVEILED IN 2004. IT RECALLS, IN LATIN, CASTILLIAN AND GALLEGO, THE HOSPITALITY EXTENDED TO PILGRIMS IN O CEBREIRO SINCE 836.

PHOTO JOAN AND JERRY COCHRANE

5

To Be A Pilgrim… This essay is drawn from Notes of a Special Meeting of the Confraternity Main Committee in June 1996. It was later published in volume 59 of the Confraternity of Saint James *Bulletin* in May 1997.

We met to discuss the fears raised by what some have seen as the recent over-promotion of the Camino de Santiago. In the face of official efforts to transform the pilgrim journey into a species of mass tourism in the Holy Year 1993, our concern was twofold: for the physical integrity of the Camino and for the quality of the pilgrim's experience of the route. We discussed whether these fears were justified, and ways of mitigating the damage and preserving the essentials. The approach of another Holy Year in 1999 made this a matter of prime importance.

As we all know, pilgrim numbers increased dramatically in 1993. We can hardly complain of that, since educating the British public about the pilgrimage and promoting interest in it through our activities is in part what the Confraternity is about. The question is whether the response to promotion, both in Spain and internationally, has actually begun to affect the character of the route. and the pilgrim's experience of it. Since the conservation of both are also among the *raisons d'être* of the Confraternity, we must consider the matter seriously.

How to safeguard the physical integrity of the route is an ongoing problem with no very clear-cut solution. The Confraternity shares the obligation to defend the historic Caminos when threats to them arise, ideally as part of a united effort with our colleagues in other countries.

In practice, it is difficult to protest if no voices are raised in Spain to give a lead. Sometimes - local interests and the press being what they are - this may happen later than it should. The best we can do is to be vigilant and as well-informed as possible, and let the *Federación de Asociaciones de Amigos del Camino de Santiago* – ' the Spanish Federation' - know of the Confraternity's support.

We must also maintain good communications with the Council of Europe and UNESCO, both of which have formally 'adopted' the Caminos. The former's commitment has taken the form of a great deal of unattractive waymarking, rather than the action that might have prevented the damage done as part of the preparation for 1993. The latter's involvement came only after the damage was done, thereby giving it a seal of approval – but they are all we have.

The effect of the pressure of numbers, and of motorised travel on the pilgrim experience, gave rise to a lengthier discussion. Since those enacting the pilgrimage in the traditional ways are now so far outstripped by car, coach and air travellers as to be in the minority, I think it is worth making a fairly basic but important distinction. The 'traditional ways' of travel – walking, cycling and on horseback -- involve using one's own decision-making and motive powers. These imply physical effort, an element of physical vulnerability, or risk, and a 'spirit', or frame of mind, that is open to enquiry, encounter, and change. For some people, this last condition means making the journey alone, or with very few companions. The 'traditional ways' also preclude, unless essential for medical reasons, the use of back-up vehicles.

The pilgrimage made in this manner and spirit is the one that qualifies for the *compostela*, whether over the minimum distance or the width of Europe. Why is the distinction so important? Perhaps it comes down to whether we accept that certain kinds of experience – solitude, silence, those spontaneous friendships that spring up among pilgrims, the everyday trials presented by geography and weather conditions – invite personal growth beyond what is offered by ordinary life. The person who embraces the vulnerable condition of the walker or the cyclist is challenged daily, and those whose aim is 'merely' to have a reasonably comfortable outdoor holiday may be challenged more than most. In other words, people attracted by the publicity surrounding the Camino and deciding to walk or cycle for purely recreational reasons, often undergo a transformation of personal values that has a lasting effect on their lives. Motorised travellers, however sincere, are less challenged by circumstances, less likely to arrive at that acceptance of dependence and inter-dependence that is one of the Camino's offerings in exchange for

Pilgrims arriving in Santiago de Compostela, 2022
photo Patti Pie Silva

physical effort. The desire to reproduce the values of the pilgrimage in daily life is the natural outgrowth of that acceptance, which must be felt in the body as well as in the mind and spirit. This acceptance resonates in the life of the walking, cycling or riding pilgrim in a way that it cannot do in the life of the traveller who is part of a coach tour.

We cannot, therefore, complain of the recent increase in the numbers of walking and cycling pilgrims out of some purist notion that many of them may not approach the pilgrimage in 'the right spirit'. The Camino has always been full of recreational travellers, and it still seems to work its considerable transformative 'magic' on a high proportion of them.

Yet it seems that numbers pose a problem in another sense. I believe that whether a pilgrimage is made on foot or in a motorised vehicle matters a great deal, for another, fundamental reason apprehended only through experience: that the pilgrim's journey is always a shared undertaking. He or she is encouraged, directed and aided by a network of 'dedicated others' -- not only those who made the pilgrim roads safe in centuries past, but today's fellow-pilgrims and guide writers, villagers and volunteers. The sustained awareness of being so supported is profoundly educative. There is also the meaningful sense of fellowship that develops among people who meet by chance as pilgrims on the Caminos, exhilaratingly free of the usual judgments and social preliminaries. Rapid, motorised travel, and travel in large groups that may be self-sufficient and have their own social dynamic, reduce the chances of having this kind of experience.

We considered whether large numbers of pilgrims on the Caminos might, over time, erode the traditional goodwill of those 'dedicated others' who live along the routes. Pilgrims often cite their interaction with local people as the most memorable experiences of their journeys. There were enough stories of pilgrims being overcharged in 1993 to suggest that the usual generosity had occasionally given way to cynicism. In that sense, the 'pilgrim experience' may already have altered, and our fears may be justified. One or two among us felt that there was no 'may' about it, and that the pressures fomented by 1993 had been decisive.

We also discussed whether, and how, those of us who go on pilgrimage could redress the balance. An obvious way is to go out of season, if planning to follow the Camino Francés, or, if the summer is the only feasible time to go, to follow one of the less-travelled routes. There will always be people for whom the Camino Francés is new, or irresistible, and for whom June to September is the only convenient time. The committee thought there were still a number of things that could be done.

First, with regard to local people, we could remind our members to be notably and unfailingly appreciative, the expression of gratitude being the hallmark of the pilgrim. (On the wall of the municipal albergue in Mansilla de las Mulas is a notice that says *And don't forget: the tourist says 'Give me...' and the pilgrim says 'thank you'.)* Tourists feel they have the 'right' to expect this or that because they are paying for it; the condition of the pilgrim claims no such 'rights' and makes no such demands. The Caminos belong to every pilgrim,

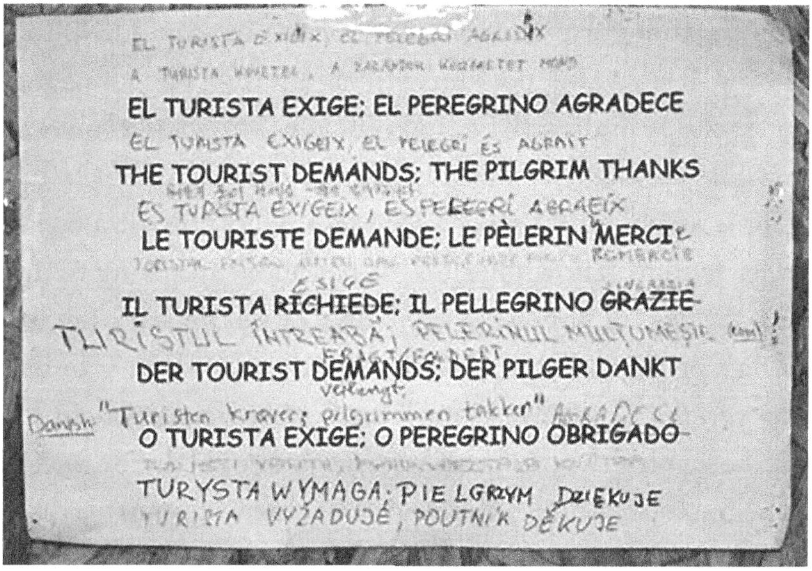

to the extent of taking responsibility for safeguarding them, but not in any personal, proprietary sense.

Secondly, we could remind our members to behave, dress and spend in a simple, discreet way that is in keeping with the most basic form of travel and the spirit of openness and encounter. That means not creating barriers between themselves and local people by offending their sensibilities. I observed two foreign pilgrims in bikinis promenading through a Galician hamlet last summer, leaving the residents scandalised; pilgrims drinking to excess has the same effect. Need we say anything about such practices as picnicking in churches, littering, using the verges of the Camino as a toilet, tempting dogs away from home, or writing graffiti?

Thirdly, and with regard to the increasing numbers of fellow-pilgrims, we thought that an attitude of service could help to dispel anonymity. It may be no more than offering encouragement to someone who is finding the going difficult. But what about carrying a bag while walking, to collect other pilgrims' litter? Or bringing along some small, useful object such as a pen-knife, or a needle and thread, to lend to fellow-pilgrims? What about resolving to do some unobtrusive act of kindness each day, or taking the initiative in gathering a group together to share experiences of the Camino?

One veteran *hospitalera* commented, after the onslaught of 1993, that the best thing the jacobean associations could do for the Camino would be to stop sending pilgrims down it. The committee disagrees.

By all means, let us keep encouraging people to make the pilgrimage to Santiago, but let us be clear about two things. Defence of the historic routes is the prime responsibility of those who claim to value them, and we must become better at speaking out. There is a real risk that in the approach to 1999, the physical Caminos will be further 'improved' by the authorities, purely for the purpose of increasing the number of people using them. I am not talking about safety measures such as the creating of alternatives to busy roads, but about such tactics as diverting a historic route through a town for commercial advantage, or widening it to make it more accessible for coaches and cars.

Secondly, we who are active in the associations must resist the growing tendency on the part of politicians to regard the Camino as a commodity, and the growing number of pilgrims and travellers as captive consumers. We can make our appreciation clear to the

Camino's army of 'dedicated others,' and encourage our members to do the same. The spirit of the Camino – its simplicity, its respectful attitude to others and to the natural world, its openness and hospitality – is part and parcel of the dedication of the people living along it. Together they have sustained the pilgrimage for a millennium. Our task, through the way we prepare our pilgrims, is to show solidarity with that spirit, to ensure that it sustains the Caminos into the next.

6

Rabanal del Camino and Refugio Gaucelmo: Why? How? When? A presentation – really, a piece of theatre - given in the crypt of St Mary Moorfields church in the City of London, on the evening of 20 June 2002

A few words of explanation:

The Confraternity, through its Rabanal Committee, was still fundraising energetically on behalf of Refugio Gaucelmo ten years after its opening. Total funds raised had just passed the £100,000 mark – more than double our original commitment - but we on that Committee sensed that the momentum was slowing. The Rabanal project needed new energy and talent. That we were missing something was brought home to us at one of our meetings, when someone suddenly said he thought there were many new members who had no idea how or why Refugio Gaucelmo had come into being, nor what it represented for the Confraternity. If that was indeed the case, then something had to be done about it.

I walked home from that meeting wondering how we could depict the story of Refugio Gaucelmo in a novel way, to capture imaginations in the way that, back at the beginning, ours had been captured. By the time I got to my own front door, an idea was taking shape, and I sat down and drafted an outline of what needed saying and who should say it. Aspects of the story would be told by each of us, in a certain order so that the overall tale unfolded clearly, but the 'lines' would be up to each participant.

The Rabanal Committee was intrigued and willing to give it a go, and a local church was happy to supply a venue. To ensure spontaneity, there was no script and no rehearsal, just a brief gathering beforehand to make sure we had the running order straight. What followed was unlike anything we'd ever done, but it certainly was entertaining, as the audio recording made by James Hatts for the CSJ Library will still remind the listener. Thanks are due to David Wesson, who later transcribed James's recording to produce the following written record, which has been very lightly edited to make it easier to read. Permission to quote the words of participants no longer with us has been sought from relatives, and granted.

LAURIE DENNETT

I walked to Santiago in 1986. It seems like yesterday in some ways and a long time ago in others. In those days the Camino was very different than it is now. There were probably only about a third of the number of *refugios* between St Jean Pied de Port and Santiago, and the impression, going through the very arid stretch of the *Montes de León* where Rabanal is situated, was one of total desolation. In Rabanal itself there was somewhere to sleep but most walkers simply skipped the section between Astorga and Ponferrada and took the train.

Refugio Gaucelmo's name recalls the saintly 12th century hermit who built a chapel and shelter for pilgrims near what is now Cruz de Ferro.

I thought that, in trying to indicate to you what things were like, I would mention two things. One is that the welcome of the people who lived along the way was just as wonderful then as now - extraordinary acts of generosity - and one perceived quickly that this was part of life for them. They had been born and spent their entire lives in these small villages. They had seen pilgrims passing in varying numbers throughout their lifetime and they never seemed to tire of them, whether they arrived early or late, summer or winter. That was one thing that struck me very forcefully on my journey.

The second thing I wanted to emphasize is the great change that has taken place in Rabanal, and I want simply to read from the book that I wrote when I came home which was called *A Hug for the Apostle.* This was what the approach to Rabanal was like in those days:

Chonina Alonso, whose family had offered hospitality to pilgrims for generations, stands near the disused parish house that became Refugio Gaucelmo
photo Paul Graham

"As the road climbed, the terrain took on a new harshness. Grass verges were gradually replaced by desiccated banks of earth, sprouting a profusion of heathers of all shades. Rocks littered the surface of the thin soil. In the twelve dusty kilometres after Santa Catalina there was only one village, El Ganso, windswept and derelict. I held my breath as we passed through. Thatched roofs had fallen inwards, stone walls collapsed. The door of a byre banged in the hot wind and made me jump. In the dirt of the road a rusting spade lay abandoned. One house had its door and window frames painted a brilliant blue suggesting

that the place had at least one resident, but dogs, that sure sign of habitation, were nowhere to be seen.

And here is Aymeric Picaud's once-prosperous ninth halt on the Way of St. James:

We reached Rabanal in mid-afternoon. Four people were sitting in the shade of a verandah facing a dusty, treeless square as we called out for directions to the Bar Chonina. This ***was*** *the Bar Chonina, and this (one of the women indicated a tanned and smiling companion) was Chonina herself. The bar, we learned, had closed in January with the imposition of the new sales tax. People here, and there were only 17 left in Rabanal, could not afford the extra few pesetas. I had secretly hoped that the bar would save us from a night in the abandoned schoolhouse. I looked around me at the poverty of the village and the hope died unspoken. ' El edificio escolar' stood across the square, windowless and listing crazily."*

I mentioned that most pilgrims skipped this section if they were on foot, because there were 50 kilometres with almost nowhere except the abandoned schoolhouse to stop in. And now – quoting again from the book – I recall the experience of sleeping in the schoolhouse:

"We picked our way across the square in the dark, sheltering a lighted candle stuck in a broken brick. Inside the schoolhouse, the floorboards had sprung free of their nails and the roof sagged. The place was filthy, thick with dust and the droppings of birds and bats. We peered about; there seemed nowhere level to unroll the sleeping-bags. Three detached doors lay against one wall; these at least would hold the floorboards down. We arranged the sleeping bags on two of them, one on either side of our packs and the candle. The mountain chill was now so extreme that I put on everything that I was not already wearing. Chonina had given me a heavy blanket, which I folded around me and crawled into my sleeping bag. The schoolroom was as black as a tomb."

As Walter Ivens will agree, that experience was a contrast to the pilgrim's experience today.

WALTER IVENS

My first visit to Rabanal was 16 years ago. It was a lovely day and we were bicycling. We had left Astorga at about nine o'clock and we arrived in Rabanal at about eleven. In fact we had stopped in front of Chonina's bar, although it was closed. This was late June so it was about a month after Laurie's trip. We pushed the bicycles to the church. Little did I realize that we were virtually opposite what was to become the *refugio*. Whilst resting by the church I walked down the actual pilgrim road and met up with an old lady sitting on her doorstep. I said "Is there any hope of buying some drink or some food?" She answered *"Hijo mio, no hay nada,"* 'My son, there is nothing.' I felt terribly chuffed by the idea of being called 'my son'. I was 58 years old and took it as a very great honour.

We then bicycled on, and my memory of Rabanal was of that old lady sitting on her doorstep. That evening after two or three glasses of red wine I wrote in my diary:

After Rabanal one passes Foncebadon and El Acebo and all three are pretty empty and derelict villages. Seeing all these derelict villages, houses tumbling down, probably still lived-in but nobody about, gave me a sense of guilt, because we, supposed pilgrims, pass by on one side with shame -- and an itch to take a photo to show off to others on the primitiveness of the camino. As modern pilgrims we take of the route, but I don't think we give back much. Yes, we spend money in hotels and bars, but these little places have nothing to offer and they can't make a profit on nothing. The early pilgrims may well have decided to return after Compostela to the places which they saw most needed help and so set up as carpenters, stonemasons and shopkeepers, and built and created to the good of the community, but we don't, and I fear the fault is ours. Maybe this will change and, like elsewhere, tourism will bring in money and with it, life, noise and laughter, and a living village again. But an empty village is an expression of sadness: 'my masters have gone away; when will they come back?'

Well, a year or so later the Confraternity was celebrating its fifth anniversary and wanted to find a future purpose for itself, and asked for proposals. So, in my proposal I quoted that text and then I went on to say:

'I would like to suggest that a purpose for the Confraternity would be to help in reviving one of these villages. We could help to convert, with care, some of the old houses into a pilgrims' hostel like the amenities and atmosphere at O Cebreiro, but also with a shop to buy provisions. Hopefully the endeavour would attract more commerce and tourism and the village will come to life.

Question: Why should the Confraternity be involved and isn't the project too big? Answer: Because we would be contributing a tangible benefit to the pilgrimage route in the form of a hostel in one of the roughest most beautiful and needy parts of the camino, a link between the past and the future. By providing the necessary services for the hostel like water, electricity, sewerage, the opportunity opens for others to settle in the village and so it provides a major step in bringing the village back to life. Such a purpose would have a great appeal, and by publicizing the appeal it would widen knowledge of the Confraternity and increase membership. The concept is big and would take years to achieve but considering it bit by bit on a lengthy timescale I believe it is within the potential of the Confraternity provided it is really considered worthwhile'.

And that was the start.

JAMES MAPLE

In the spring of 1988, the committee decided to ask for suggestions. Any organization that is going to thrive needs good ideas from people. The original group who started the Confraternity had a brilliant idea and they saw it through – a good idea needs carrying through. We had several suggestions; we were delighted with Walter's idea, but as with all ideas, somebody has to do something about it. With this we had a good team, but Walter and Mary did a vast amount of the work. (Walter hates me saying that. So does Mary).

What we did was write to the Federation of the Spanish Associations of *Amigos del Camino*, who were our opposite numbers in Spain, and we said that we would like to do this, and we left it to the Federation to tell us where our project was most needed. We gave them an outline of our ideas for a *refugio* of some sort, but we didn't say where because we didn't feel we had the right to.

Now that letter was written in the spring, and in the summer we had still heard nothing, but then of course this was Spain, where things moved more slowly. But in October we heard that there was something happening, and in February 1989 we had a letter from somebody who will be known to quite a lot of you, Alberto Morán, who was a priest in Molinaseca and secretary of the Amigos of El Bierzo. He wrote with the news that the Bishop of Astorga had ceded the parish house in Rabanal to his association and ours to make into a *refugio*. It was apparently nearly a complete ruin, and he hoped we could restore it some way. The main committee approved the whole idea. But it was a smaller committee, the Rabanal committee, that got it all going.

Pat Quaife (Confraternity Chair), Joe May (Co-Ordinator) and Walter Ivens (Project Manager) survey the patio of the future Refugio Gaucelmo
photo Paul Graham

Laurie Dennett

When we heard from Alberto Morán in February 1989, we arranged to make an exploratory visit. The first three deputised to go were Walter Ivens, Paul Graham and myself. We went in May, for a long weekend. We flew to Santiago, rented a car and got ourselves to Ponferrada, where we met for the first time our colleagues of the *Amigos del Camino de El Bierzo*. These were four in number: Don Luis Bacariza, a doctor, very well known in the area since he'd looked after Rabanal, and who was at that time President of the *Amigos*. He was a very imposing man, rather reserved, but he knew a lot of people and I think it was probably through him that the Bishop had been led to make this gesture. Secondly, Don Alberto Morán: many of you know how delightful he is! Instant sunshine, very enthusiastic, full of music, very friendly - and he made us feel immediately at home. There were two others: one called Paco, who was the treasurer, and one called Eulogio, whom we came to call 'El Greco', since he was an artist. He was also a metalworker, and by the way, it was he who created the monument to the German pilgrim who was killed on his bicycle in El Acebo. (As you come out of El Acebo the monument is on your left).

We had supper with them on the Friday evening, and on the Saturday morning they introduced us to Rogelio Valcarce, who was the builder, or *contratista*, who would be in charge of the project. He took us to see three houses which he had restored. They were all very beautiful, like chalets, and we were duly impressed.

We were then taken to see the ruin in Rabanal. I think they were trying to buffer us against the shock, and it was quite a shock! The building was in an unbelievable state. The entire interior had collapsed, and there was a hole in the front wall that you could have driven a bus through. (We made another flying visit a few months later, and between the two visits the roof saved us half a million pesetas by collapsing inwards, so we didn't have to go to the trouble of taking it down. The great beam which had been holding it up just

Refugio Gaucelmo came into being stage by stage, as funds were raised in the UK and work in Rabanal could be undertaken and paid for

collapsed, and we may have been taking a risk on that first visit by walking around under it.) But even though it was derelict, the place was quite something. Paul, Walter and I returned to our hotel after another convivial dinner with the *Amigos* and sat up half the night, deciding whether we ought to involve the Confraternity in this, or run a mile. The commitment was for ten million pesetas, which was at that point about £50,000. The Confraternity had fewer than 500 members and it seemed an incredible thing to be embarking on, but in the end we decided that yes, it was something with our name written on it. It was just something we were called to do. We came away fully convinced that this was our Camino, as it were.

Walter Ivens

We were trembling with fear at the idea of how to raise £50,000. What we had not anticipated was this incredible sense of giving — in fact it is mostly giving back -- because the giving was mostly done by people who'd been pilgrims, and so knew all about hospitality on the Camino. This giving took place in donations; it also took place through individuals using their talents to raise money. It took place in actual work, as in working parties or work as wardens. It covered the UK, but we had help from European associations, we had help from America, and we had help especially from Spain. Spain provided the bunks and the kitchen furniture. And we had special help from Alberto Morán, the man who got things going. If it hadn't been for Alberto I don't think there'd have been a *refugio*. He was incredible. So it was this sense of giving... if we talk of how the *refugio* was created, the answer is through everyone's giving.

Mary Ivens

I'm going to say something about fund raising. I know it's a dull subject but I'll try and make it as light as I can. Fundraising is a daunting task at the best of times. To try and raise money to build a pilgrims' hostel in northern Spain was a huge challenge. Mention the

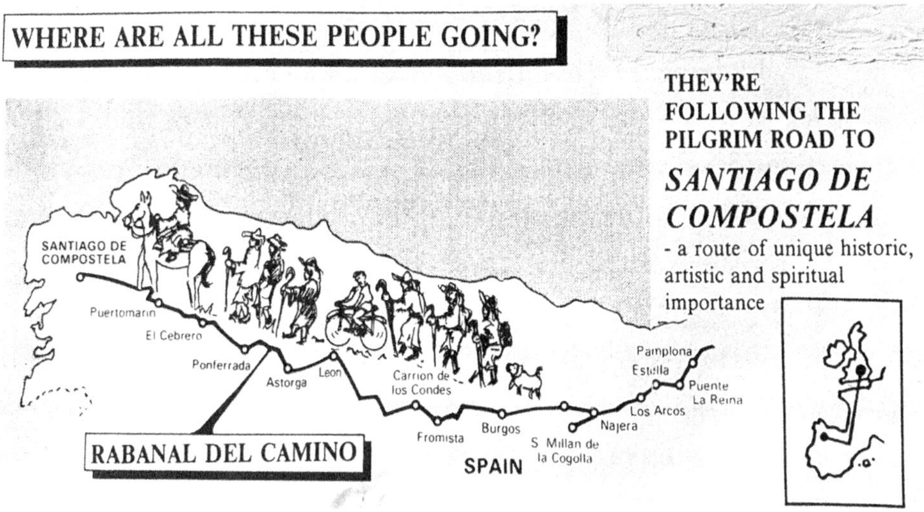

idea to anyone and you either received a glazed look and a "Where's that? On the Costa?" or else a gleam of interest and "Santiago de what?"

So in September 1989 we produced a leaflet and called it "Where are all these people going?" and a mug to match. Our honorary President, the Spanish Ambassador, agreed to help us launch the campaign in November 1989 with a party at the Spanish Embassy.

Invitations were sent out and somehow the news reached a man called Jésus Jato. Some of you may have met him in Villafranca. He is one of the Camino's great characters, who had been offering hospitality to pilgrims all his life. He made his way from Villafranca to London, and to everyone's surprise he turned up at the Embassy two hours early. He was told firmly to sit in the entrance hall until somebody could vouch for him. Alberto Morán was there too, and a 'cheque of hope,' but no money, was ceremonially handed over to him by James Hatts, aged eight, in front of the party.

Now our membership at that time was around 500. We needed £50,000, which meant £100 from each member, which really was an unrealistic sum. But an early success was an offer from the Bernard Sunley Foundation to contribute £2,500 every time we reached a £10,000 mark, amounting to £10.000 in all. Members and friends gave generously over the years, with sums that went from one pound to hundreds. As Walter said, various other charities contributed, and some of the European associations made donations. We had to devise ways of raising money ourselves.

Phinella Henderson, a CSJ member, raised £800 by doing a sponsored parachute jump, which frightened the life out of us. She then offered to do a bungee jump which we turned down as being far too dangerous. (Walter remembers that she went ahead anyway and did it for another charity.) Another member, Ted Dickinson, did gardening locally and every penny he earned went to the appeal and gained much needed publicity.

In those days there was little interest in the Camino. The media hadn't yet discovered it, so there were no TV films, no books. Adrian Wright ran a sponsored London Marathon in 1990, and CSJ founder member Mary Remnant gave lecture recitals with her marvellous collection of mediaeval musical instruments. One of the biggest things we did was to hold a raffle in 1990 with an Evans bicycle as the first prize. The second prize was a beautiful scallop shell quilt made by Loella Hanbury-Tenison, the wife of the well-known traveller.

In May of the same year Paul Graham, supported by various CSJ members, took his famous penny farthing bicycle to Bath where he had the idea of riding it up and down in the square in front of the abbey with a tin for money clipped on the handlebars. This he did most successfully, and we went round trying to explain to passers-by what it was all about. We collected the princely sum of £14, and one button. Not all our efforts were successful, but we did enjoy ourselves. The following year a weekend was organised in Norfolk, where a member's friend had built a miniature railway and the money charged for rides went into the appeal.

Not all the fundraising was tough going. Paul organized a wine-tasting evening which was very well attended by members. We sat at tables on which was a paper describing the various wines we were going to taste. The corks popped, the wine was poured and we tasted... and we tasted... and we tasted... too well. Ignoring the correct procedure of spitting a mouthful of the wine into the bucket provided, we swallowed every drop. By the time we reached the last two bottles I could remember absolutely nothing of the pedigree, where it came from, the flavour, the colour. We enjoyed ourselves, and I think that is one of the things I must make clear about the fundraising; dreary subject though it may seem: we had an enormous amount of fun.

One morning at breakfast during the appeal Walter and I were worried about how we could find £100 to pay an essential Rabanal bill. We were stumped for an idea and Walter started to open our post. To our amazement a cheque for just that sum floated out of an envelope with an English stamp. Apart from a signature we never knew who our kind donor was. I think that was a little bit of Saint James helping us along the way. We hit the £50,000 target in under two years, and today the figure raised is around £110,000.

'Santiago Peregrino', carved by the English sculptor Beauford Linley, welcomes pilgrims to Refugio Gaucelmo
photo Joseph May

In 1988 I found a sculptor to make a small statue of a pilgrim Saint James for Walter's 60th birthday. Beauford Linley lived in a small cottage south of Grantham with his wife and an enormous Irish wolfhound, and numerous cats and a goat in the back garden. Beauford knew nothing about Saint James, but happily created the birthday present. Now when a generous benefactor donated a sum for a statue of Saint James to be made in memory of Father Elias Valiña, Beauford set to in the piggeries on his smallholding to make a metre-high statue in an English stone known as 'Ancaster White'. Today that statue stands in a niche in the façade of *Refugio Gaucelmo*, watching the pilgrims come and go through Rabanal and in and out of the *refugio*. I think Joe May has a story to tell about the statue's installation.

A TENSE BUT TRIUMPHANT MOMENT, AS A CRANE LOWERS THE STATUE OF ST JAMES INTO HIS NICHE IN THE FACADE

JOSEPH MAY

I was with Walter and Mary when we picked up the statue, and I promised Beauford that I would see it placed in position myself. We then put it in the back of the van and proceeded to Rabanal. One of the minor snags was that none of us knew whether it was legal to take works of art out of the country without saying something to somebody, and we certainly didn't know whether it was legal to import works of art into Spain, again without saying something to somebody. We decided to put that question out of our minds and wrapped Saint James up quite comfortably in some sleeping bags. The party decided that I should be the driver since I had the most honest face.

What they really meant was that I was the most plausible rogue. One thing that we should all remember about that statue is that it is there in memory of Don Elias Valiña, the parish priest of O Cebreiro, the great scholar of the *Camino* and the man who marked it with yellow arrows to give the whole idea of the pilgrimage a lift and a sense of direction.

The erection of the statue was quite interesting, because there were a couple of stainless-steel rods sticking out of the bottom. Those stainless-steel rods had to be fitted into holes in the niche, and I drilled the holes. The day came when it was all going to happen. The builders had brought a crane and the whole of the square was filled with everybody from the village. The slightly daunting thing from my point of view was that every one of them knew as absolute fact that the statue wouldn't fit into that niche. My friend Jésus, who lived in Rabanal, helped me. Eventually we got it into position. He put in the waterproof cement at the bottom and sealed it all. I have inspected the statue every year, with two exceptions, since it was installed, and the sealing hasn't changed one jot or tittle in all that time. The statue may well be unique, because it is the only statue of Saint James as far as I know that was erected by Joseph and Jésus.

The other thing worth describing are the working parties. The very first of the working parties, in the spring of 1990, was almost a site-clearing job, brutally hard work and not all the members of the party were used to sustained manual labour. Once again our friend Alberto saved our bacon. The house that his parents were going to occupy in Molinaseca was vacant, so he offered it to us. We worked in the daytime on the *refugio,* and then we drove over the hills to Molinaseca

Left to right, the Confraternity's first working party, autumn 1989, accompanied by 'Ublines' (Rabanal's sacristan), on far left: Walter Ivens, Maurice Morgan, Alberto Moran, Roger Tisseau, John Durant, Jonathan Ingham.

and stayed in the house. So we were able to sleep comfortably, and warmly and recover properly so as to be fit for the next day's work. The only problem was that the house didn't have any doors, so there was a marked shortage of privacy. If we wanted for any reason to go to one of the small rooms we had to sit and whistle, just to make sure we weren't interrupted.

During that first working party we had our first pair of pilgrims, a Scots couple. We were up to our eyes in dust and dirt when this pair walked in. They walked straight up to me and said, "What can

Paul Murray, author of a commemorative history of Refugio Gaucelmo, with Etienne and Nelly Van Wonterghem-Tierlinck, from Belgium, its first wardens

we do to help?" and if that doesn't epitomise the spirit of the *Camino* I don't know what does. I promptly gave them each a broom and said "Go upstairs and clear the floor," and that was how the floor of the *dormitorio* was cleared. After their labours of the day we couldn't turn them out, and we couldn't take them to Molinaseca, so we said "We'll make you up a bed," which we did in one of the small rooms. We had a large number of polystyrene insulation sheets which we piled up, and then we said, "There you are, get on that, that's the best insulated and warmest bed in Spain!" I have never forgotten those two, and their very first words: "What can we do to help?" It was a wonderful thing.

For quite a long time after the refugio actually opened, I was involved in organising the wardens rota. Wardens came from all over the world: from the United States, from Norway, from Holland, Belgium, Switzerland, the UK... you name it, they came. They came at their own expense, they worked exceedingly hard, and still do, to make the pilgrims comfortable. We have been truly blessed because they have done a wonderful job. On one occasion as a cycling pilgrim I arrived at Rabanal on Saint James' day, and lo and behold, the wardens were Peter and Eileen FitzGerald. So now I know exactly what it is like to be royalty and arrive in a strange place, because they looked after me better than anyone has ever looked after me (my wife excluded!). Our wardens have done a magnificent job and we must all be very grateful. In the years I was organising them I had very, very few problems to deal with.

One other thing: Etienne and Nelly, who were the first wardens, and David Wesson, who succeeded them, and was quite frequently a warden subsequently, set the pattern in many ways, and in those early days did something that was crucial to the development and the character of Rabanal. We had already decided that the refuge would operate on the basis of pilgrims' donations, but these wardens added the idea that pilgrims were to be sent off in the morning with breakfast, and we would leave it to them to put into the donations box whatever they thought was appropriate. It has been an immense success. I've seen people standing by the donations box just stuffing in notes out of sheer gratitude for the way they have been looked after, and for the special magic that *Refugio Gaucelmo* bestows on pilgrims. It is the wardens that we should thank, because they have kept the breakfasts going all these years.

Paul Graham

What Joe didn't mention was that he actually made the donations box with a very large hole at the top for very large bank notes.

Joseph May

When I told my local wood yard what I wanted it for, they gave me a lovely plank of English oak to make it with, and of course, they donated it to the *refugio*. Yet another example of generosity from people with no knowledge of the Camino.

Paul Graham

At the inauguration of the refugio in October 1991 there were pilgrims, the villagers and the Maragato dancers. It was quite simply an expression of how faith in the project had in fact triumphed at that stage. Some seasoned fundraisers had predicted that we might raise two to three thousand pounds altogether towards our £50,000, and eventually we were very glad to have raised over £100,000. The inauguration celebrated by the Bishop of Astorga was an international meeting. People from the British Embassy in Madrid came, and many friends from other organisations to do with the *Camino*. It was appropriate that it should be an international meeting, because this was not an English *refugio*. It was an international *refugio,* and from the beginning it has been celebrated as such.

Marion Marples

There were really two patterns of activity. There was the work going on in Spain with the El Bierzo Association and the builders

Open doors at last

and organising the wardens, while all the time, at home in England (and I was one of those who was very much at home) there was the fund raising, about which Mary has told some of the highlights.

One of the other features was a typewritten A4 leaflet 'Rabanal News' which came out with every *Bulletin*, encouraging people to continue raising money, sharing ideas, listing donors on the back, and challenging people to find more and more ingenious ways in which they could contribute. It soon became apparent that our Number One ideas man was none other than Paul Graham here. At the end of a Rabanal sub-committee meeting - I find it extraordinary that anything happened as a result of these meetings because they were always well-fuelled with a couple of bottles of wine and Mary would produce a tray of sandwiches and we'd all have a very splendid and convivial evening - right at the end Paul would always say "I have an idea." To which, unfortunately, I usually said "No, I don't think it's a good idea." I dubbed those four words 'the most dangerous four words in the English language'.

I have to hand it to Paul that many of his ideas were extremely successful. One of his ideas, right at the beginning, was that we should have a symbol for the appeal through which we could show the progress we were making. Other appeals used staircases, thermometers and so on, but we had a map of the *Camino*. Fortuitously the Camino is 500 miles long, and we were trying to raise £50,000, so one mile equalled £100. It was thought that we should ask somebody, or have a competition, to draw a little figure that could move along the map of the Camino to show where we had got to in our appeal. John Durant of Bristol drew a beautiful little Maragato drummer, and as the money came in the drummer moved along the Camino. That was a very handy relationship for the £50,000 but we had an interim target of £35,000, 350 miles, and Rabanal is 350 miles from Roncesvalles, so we could make him get to Rabanal and that was our first target, and anything else would go with the momentum perhaps of fund raising. The drummer actually moved very speedily, helped by donations like the Bernard Sunley Foundation's, and so on. He was a very successful little mascot.

Paul's other brilliant idea was 'Sponsor a Week.' It was good for people who couldn't go parachuting, or couldn't do gardening, or who couldn't get out to Rabanal, but would still like to be involved. The year could be divided up into weeks, and people could pick the week of their birthday, wedding anniversary or whatever, and choose to sponsor that week. As a thank-you they would receive a letter from the current warden detailing what had been happening in the refuge that week. I know that all the people who have participated in this scheme have really valued the contact, often on an annual basis now. Initially it was for one year, but it has continued ever since. It provides a very useful source of regular income, and has provided much pleasure to those taking part.

Apart from funds raised, Rabanal has also received many donations in kind. It has almost got to the stage now where one rather worries about people - members of the Confraternity – dying, because there is some form of bequest, something else to be put up in Rabanal, and we don't want it to become a mausoleum. Some of the early gifts, however, were very welcome, and much appreciated. Not as any kind of legacy, Peter FitzGerald made a statue of Saint James to grace the inside of the *refugio*, which was a wonderful gift. Aileen O'Sullivan gave money to buy trees for the *huerta* and they have been nurtured and just about survived. We have acquired a number of works of art of variable quality, which sometimes we have to move around so we don't have them quite as prominently visible as they might be. The big table with integral benches in the salon was given in memory of a member. These gifts have all been important for the building up of the furnishing and comfort of the refuge. The final big donation, which was very much appreciated, is the icon of *Santiago Peregrino,* which was blessed in 2001 on the tenth anniversary of the opening. It was given in memory of Stephen Badger, who as Treasurer of the Confraternity was very influential in the raising of funds -- as was his successor Timothy Wotherspoon.

Other help we received from the *Madrileñas*, the two ladies from Madrid who lived next door to the refuge. They were endlessly helpful to us, in that they were able to organise and chivvy workmen for us, and take delivery of various items of equipment. They were responsible for immensely improving the wardens' bathroom, and contributing to the general wellbeing of the working parties whenever they were there. Wonderful people, Asumpta and Charo, who have now moved away, but keep in touch.

All this goodness and help, enterprise and inspiration going into *Refugio Gaucelmo* has spilled over into the village. Going back to Rabanal now we see that the main road is paved instead of being rough and stony and muddy in winter. The houses, instead of being like the ones Laurie described with the roofs falling in, are having new roofs put on them. Families are not necessarily coming back to live in Rabanal the whole year, but they are coming back in the summer months. On my last visit, for the tenth anniversary, I was immeasurably moved by the fact that there were large numbers of children in the village again. We hadn't seen children in the village before. A school party was bewitched by William Griffiths in his pilgrim hat and cloak, and intrigued by the whole pilgrim phenomenon.

LAURIE DENNETT

In December 1996 a very wonderful thing occurred. The fifth anniversary of the official opening of *Refugio Gaucelmo* had just passed in late October, and in December the Confraternity was the first recipient of an honour called the *Premio Elias Valiña*. I should add a bit to what Joe said about Elias Valiña himself. He was the parish priest of O Cebreiro for 30 years and the person who brought the Camino back to life in modern times. He wrote the first really practical guides to it, he knew it inch by inch, and knew it better than anyone. He was one of those extraordinary people who is remembered more and more – not less and less – as time goes by. He was a person of tremendous self-giving - he was never too tired to talk to pilgrims, to look after pilgrims, to make whatever he had available to them. He was, as Joe said, a great scholar, but he was also exceedingly practical. He did his best to create facilities for pilgrims that were not only dignified, but that would foster the spirit of the Camino, encourage people from different countries to get together and get to know one another, to talk together in the evenings beside the log fire in O Cebreiro. He was a wonderful priest, and one of the significant personalities on the Camino.

When he died in 1989, it was rather difficult to decide how to commemorate such a person. Some of his friends who had been appointed to the *Xunta de Galicia's* Committee of Camino Experts persuaded the *Xunta* to institute the *Elias Valiña Prize*. It was to be awarded to the association, or the individual, whose activities on behalf of pilgrims best epitomised the spirit of the Camino. It was a tremendous joy and honour for the Confraternity to win it in the very first year it was awarded. I was present in Santiago on that day in December 1996, and accepted the award on behalf of the Confraternity. I think everyone who voted for us was simply saying 'thank you' to the members of the Confraternity, who had worked together to create this wonderful *refugio*.

Another of the beautiful things about *Refugio Gaucelmo* is that it has inspired the associations of other countries. The Italians were very shortly behind us in restoring the ruins of San Nicolás at Puente Fitero. I don't know whether any of you have ever stayed there, but it's unforgettable. It has no electricity, everything is done by candlelight, the wardens wash the pilgrims' feet on arrival and everyone shares whatever food they have. It is always a memorable experience for the pilgrims who stay there. The Swiss are at Belorado, and an individual Swiss donor has endowed the large new albergue at Ponferrada. The Germans have now established one small *refugio* at Azofra and another two in Hospital de Orbigo and Foncebadon, and a German cultural organisation has now set up one at La Faba. All of them have cited the example of the Confraternity in doing what they have done. I think that cannot help but move us all.

Mary Ivens

I am no carpenter, I am no electrician, and I'm not much use with a paintbrush, but one of the main things about a working party week is that you have to keep warm. These working parties are at the end of March, and as you all know, at the end of March there is still snow around, and sometimes when we went there was snow in Rabanal. I remember one of my first times not realising just how cold it was trotting along to the bathroom with my sponge bag, pyjamas, and dressing gown, finding everything in thick snow. Another time we had the most fantastic weather and we were worrying about peoples' sun-burnt noses or trying to find old straw hats because it was so incredibly hot. You never knew what the weather was going to be like and you had to be prepared for everything.

I found myself in the position of housekeeper, really, because everybody started work after breakfast at half past eight and they worked jolly hard and by the time they got to the Spanish time for lunch at about two o'clock, everyone was extremely hungry. I have to say that most times when I went we had lunch outside in the patio on the wobbly old benches and equally wobbly old table and it was absolutely marvellous. Those that were there will remember the stories and the wine, and not everyone worked that hard in the afternoon! One of the things that somebody in the working party has to do is to go into Astorga and buy provisions. In the evenings they went alternately to Antonio's and to Chonina's for a hot supper, but lunch and breakfast had to be bought. Tuesday is market day in Astorga and it was enormous fun to return with lots of things in the back of the car, not quite sure what some of them were.

There is in the hall an antique bench in memory of John Halliday and it fell to me to clean it up and to polish it. To my horror I realised it was full of woodworm. This was many years ago, so it was treated, and it was polished and it was put back. After all this time when I went back this year I asked some strong gentleman to turn it over and found the same old woodworm still there! But it is still a lovely old bench for pilgrims to sit on, perhaps whilst they are waiting to sign in.

Joseph May

Well, I've got the remains of a lot of blisters. I think the thing about the working parties is that they were made up of volunteers and there are a certain amount of building and decorating skills that you need when you are doing things to a place like *Refugio Gaucelmo*. The great thing that I will always remember is how Walter and I used to go into Astorga to visit either the ironmonger or the man who sells the paints and decorating things. If we were to walk in there now, they would do what they have been doing for years past: they would welcome us like brothers. They were always pleased to see us, they always gave us a pilgrim discount, and I reckon we got the best deals. The thing about all working parties is that everyone brought along a skill, and all the work was undertaken in the same spirit of giving something back to the *Camino*, and it worked exceedingly well. As Mary said, at times it was very, very cold. In fact the weather was the enemy on many working parties, but the work was done and we had an annual opportunity to be sure that the *refugio* was up to scratch.

Paul Graham

I will bring the story up to date now so that we can conclude.

About three years ago a community of three Benedictine monks moved into the house next door that used to be lived in by the *Madrileñas*, who have now gone to Seville. They sing some parts of the Liturgy of the Hours in the church every day, and they are very popular with the pilgrims. They have added to the attraction of Rabanal as a staging post for those on the Camino.

Sister Petra Clare's icon, commissioned by the Confraternity in memory of its first treasurer, Stephen Badger - a tireless fundraiser on behalf of Refugio Gaucelmo. photo James Maple

Another of our fundraising efforts was the Tower Appeal. None of what we have tried to do would have succeeded without the help of the villagers, so we wanted to find a way of saying 'thank you' to them. We learned that the belfry of the church needed renovation, or in fact replacement. We went to the Bishop of Astorga and said to him 'We will contribute towards the renovation of the belfry'. He said 'Thank you very much,' and so we set about another Appeal. This meant another leaflet and more effort, but astonishingly we managed to raise £8000 in precisely three months. In October 1999 the Bishop came to Rabanal and blessed the restored tower, and there was yet another party.

At the end of 1999 several of those I call the "principal pioneers" of the project retired from the Rabanal committee. Walter and Mary Ivens, Pat Quaife, Joe May and James Maple stood down, and to remember their extraordinary efforts, and those of the others involved from the beginning, we are this year installing in the *refugio* four or five panels, each in a different language, describing how the *refugio* came about, and inviting pilgrims to enjoy it. The text that we propose to put on the perspex panels is:

'This pilgrim hostel was rebuilt from ruins by the Confraternity of Saint James and the Amigos del Camino de Santiago de El Bierzo as a gift to the Way of Saint James and all who travel it. The imagination, physical labour, and love of many people made it possible and continue to sustain it. We, the pioneers of both associations, hope that you will find here the peace and happiness that will strengthen you for your onward journey to the City of the Apostle. In the meadow you will find a pergola placed there to commemorate the tenth anniversary of the Refugio Gaucelmo and to offer you rest and tranquillity'.

Asociación de Amigos del Camino de Santiago de El Bierzo
Confraternity of Saint James
Refugio Gaucelmo - Rabanal del Camino
016
062
091
112
PILAS USADAS
USED BATTERIES

A spaghetti supper for everyone,
prepared by a group of Italian pilgrims.
photo Julie Davies

Refugio Gaucelmo's tranquil garden is often the setting for pilgrims to share a meal.
PHOTO JULIE DAVIES

Then we give the full names of the two associations: *'The Rabanal Committee of the Amigos del Camino de Santiago de El Bierzo and The Rabanal Committee of the Confraternity of Saint James'* - and I insisted on putting this - *'inspired by Walter Ivens'*.

Last October (2001) we celebrated the tenth anniversary of the inauguration, and many CSJ members came on a visit. The villagers were there, members of other associations all came, the Bishop celebrated Mass, and again we had a party in the *huerta*. Also in October the 60,000th pilgrim arrived. He happened to be a man from Zaragoza who arrived at the *refugio* on 12 October, the *Dia del Pilar* and the patronal feast of Zaragoza, so he was very pleased.

The best drummer in the Maragateria,
Maximiliano Arce, a Rabanal resident.

As an afterword to this account, it's worth mentioning that a slightly shortened version of it was re-enacted on 9 July 2016 at the celebration of the 25th anniversary of the refugio's opening. Other 'actors' stood in for Walter Ivens and Joe May, both of whom had died, and for James Maple, who was unable to attend. The rest of us were there, and read our parts with added enthusiasm. It was a wonderful weekend, with concerts, a Mass of thanksgiving, and a party in the huerta, complete with a splendid buffet prepared by acting hospitaleros Bob and Rowena Macdonald. Among those present were some 40 CSJ members, a number of pilgrims and several hospitaleros, past and present, members of the Amigos del Camino de El Bierzo, the diocese of Astorga, the Benedictine community of San Salvador de Monte Irago, friends such as Alberto and Eulalia Aza, Charo Carrion and Asumpta Oriol (the Madrileñas'), D. Alberto Morán, Rogelio Valcarce, and of course, the residents of Rabanal, now numbering more than 70, together with the local troupe of musicians and dancers.

A further adaptation by Sue Hemmings was read online, via Zoom, on 25 October 2021, to mark the 30th anniversary of the opening of Refugio Gaulcelmo in 1991.

7

European Pilgrims Today (and the Associations that make it all possible) A talk given at the Galería Sargadelos, Santiago de Compostela, 7 October 2003

Before I begin, I'd like to express my thanks for the opportunity of speaking to you this evening, and to convey to you the good wishes of the association I represent, the Confraternity of Saint James, based in London, which celebrates its twentieth anniversary this year. We are happy and proud to form part of the 'family' of jacobean associations that today extends around the world, for which Compostela continues to be not only the reference point, but also the head and heart.

My most vivid experience of the Camino de Santiago derives mainly from walking here as a pilgrim in the spring of 1986. Looking back over the years, I have moments when that morning when I said farewell to the French city of Chartres, setting off for Compostela in the driving rain, seems like yesterday. There are other moments when I feel that, yes, many years have passed, and the Camino I came to know back then no longer exists. None the less, I am convinced that even if the physical Camino has altered forever, the living and unifying experiences of the journey continue, especially that essential aspect that we call 'the spirit of the Camino.' The Camino spirit survives, despite the diverse changes and innovations of our time, from roadworks and 'massification' to new technologies and their social effects. It links pilgrims to one another, and each to the long history of the pilgrimage through the centuries.

My first 'Camino' proved to be the prelude to two more pilgrim journeys. In 1989 I made another pilgrimage, this time from my home in London to Rome. Then, in 1992, I made a third, from Canterbury to Jerusalem. I'm convinced that had I not first had that sustaining experience of pilgrimage along the Camino Francés, I never would have walked to Rome or to Jerusalem. The popular awareness of pilgrimage on the routes leading to those great spiritual centres had long been forgotten, and today's network of practical support did not yet exist, so the going was at times quite hard. On neither of those routes was I ever recognised as a pilgrim until I was almost within sight of my destination. The astounded Franciscan friar to whom I presented myself on arrival in Jerusalem had never met a pilgrim who had actually *walked* there. Those he usually met, numbering in the thousands every year, arrived in planes or ships, then tour-buses. He was speechless as I showed him my collection of dated stamps, set out in rows on ordinary sheets of paper, since there was, at that time, no equivalent of the Camino's *credencial*.

The author, standing in the ruins of the priory at Gradignan, just south of Bordeaux.
photo Odile Dern

For that sense of the jacobean pilgrimage's long, unbroken history, and for many other reasons, it is always a pleasure to be back in Santiago, and to share reflections about this fascinating and illuminating journey. To speak of the pilgrimage implies speaking about pilgrims. Obviously, the ones I know best are those from the British Isles, many of whom are members of the Confraternity, on whom I will centre part of this talk. But I will also try to keep faith with the title that has drawn you here this evening: *European Pilgrims Today* with its subtitle, *and their Associations*. How is their experience the same, or different, from that of pilgrims in times past? What is it that inspires and enables them in ever-increasing numbers? And what influence might their collective experience have in the Europe of today and tomorrow?

The city of Santiago, where all the Caminos converge, has a unique perspective from which to view the great network of routes that links it with countries on the frontiers of Europe. To pilgrims coming from that far away, this perspective is reversed: all roads lead to one single point on the map, and it draws them like a magnet: the longed-for City of the Apostle. I'm sure that today, as in times past, any resident of Compostela who meets a pilgrim from Norway or Bulgaria, or who learns that someone has set off from their own front door in Normandy, experiences a sense of disbelief that is almost dizzying. 'Walk all that way? How is that possible?' (The pilgrim himself may have felt, months ago in his own country, on first hearing about the pilgrimage: 'Walk all that way? How is that possible?')

Here in Santiago, you see pilgrims arriving, day after day, month after month, year after year, as they have arrived and been seen through the centuries. The statistics so carefully gathered and analysed each year by the Pilgrim Office have put solid numbers to the recent enormous growth of the pilgrimage – something that few people need convincing of, especially here in the streets around the cathedral. The largest percentage of pilgrims – some 63 per cent in 2002 – continue to be from Spain, as has always been the case. Spanish pilgrims are not that far from home, they speak – although sometimes with different accents – the same language, and share the same social customs.

But the statistics also show us the trends, the gradual and interesting changes over the past decade.

Among those trends is the growing number of pilgrims from outside Spain, who each year form a larger percentage of the overall total: just over 20 per cent in 1993, some 33 per cent in 1999, and 37 per cent in 2002. The majority of these are European, but wherever they come from, they are encouraging proof of the widely felt longing, especially among the young, to seek a profound and positive meaning for their lives, and to do so by setting out for Compostela. Behind these figures are individuals, each with his or her own language, beliefs, culture and customs. Each has an interior disposition, with all its light and shadows, an experience of the world, and a reservoir of hopes and uncertainties. How has this diverse collection of people from all over the Continent, and from even farther afield, arrived at the common paths across Spain that lead to Compostela?

In the stations of London's famous underground transport system, 'the Tube,' when the train stops and the doors slide open, a disembodied voice enjoins those alighting to 'Mind the Gap' – which is to say, 'Take care' or 'Watch out' for the space between the train and the platform. This 'gap' between the conveyance and a solid platform seems to me to offer a little metaphor for the desire of the pilgrim from some far-off country to 'arrive at' Compostela, and his need to pay attention to the large 'gap' that lies between this desire and its realisation.

The pilgrim's desire to set out on the Camino may arise from many sources, but in the weeks and months before departure, these varied motivations become subsumed in the common task of preparation. Every would-be pilgrim needs to become well-informed before that intention can be turned into reality. The entities that fill the 'gap' between desire and destination are the Associations that in other countries bear names equivalent to Spain's *Amigos del Camino de Santiago*. For the majority of European pilgrims, their first solid information comes through contact with these Associations, so their work is of prime importance.

It's probably speculating about chickens and eggs to try to determine whether the numbers of pilgrims from beyond the Pyrenees has increased thanks to the efforts of these Associations, or whether the Associations have multiplied in response to the Camino becoming 'fashionable' due to other, more publicity-related factors. In recent years, both Spain and the Camino de Santiago as a specific destination have been widely promoted internationally. The first of the large campaigns to publicise the Camino was mounted in 1991 by the Xunta de Galicia, in the run-up to the 1993 Compostellan Holy Year. At about the same time, Spanish Tourist Offices around the world were highlighting the country's many other attractions, and these promotions, too, sometimes had the effect of sparking interest in the Camino. Returning for a moment to the London Tube trains, I recall from about 10 years ago a series of posters depicting the landscapes, towns and vineyards of Navarre, that were striking enough to prompt telephone enquiries to the Confraternity.

Whatever it is that gets a pilgrim onto the Road, and quite apart from any promotional campaign, the national Associations are the great providers of information and practical support in the European countries. Their origins are part of the history of the rebirth of the pilgrimage in modern times. As is well known, the first of those Associations, the *Société des Amis de Saint Jacques de Compostelle*, was established in Paris, France, in 1950. As the only organisation of this kind until the first Spanish one was founded in Estella in 1962, and then as the only one outside Spain, the *Société* was the source which almost everyone wishing to make the pilgrimage to Compostela relied on for more than 30 years.

The big change came with the 1982 Holy Year, with the publication by Spain's Ministry of Tourism of its first *Guia del Peregrino al Camino de Santiago.* Illustrated with maps, it was compiled by a team led by Don Elías Valiña Sampedro, whose name will be familiar to most of you here this evening. This guidebook was distributed throughout Spain itself, and throughout the world via Spanish embassies and consulates. The book presented its readers with the physical traces of the pilgrimage in all their beauty and ancient glory, but with the clear message that the path that linked these places and monuments should be walked or cycled, and not just read about. With its second edition in 1985, the *Guía* reached an even wider Spanish public, as news vendors and petrol stations were persuaded to stock it.

It's well known, especially here in Galicia, how much the renaissance of the pilgrimage to Santiago owes to Don Elías. What is possibly less well known is his renown as a pioneer in the rest of Europe. From the 1960s onwards his research brought him in touch with a number of foreign scholars working in Spain who shared his passion for the Camino. Several of them, on returning to their own countries, set up groups to continue study and promotion of the Way. Professor Paolo Caucci von Saucken from Perugia (then teaching at the University here in Santiago, and today President of the Xunta de Galicia's Committee of Experts on the Camino), founded in Italy in 1982 the first of these: the *Centro di Studi Compostellani*, together with a *Confraternitá* dedicated to San Giacomo, or St James. Similarly, Dr. Robert Plötz, following a year's sabbatical in Oviedo, established the *Deutsches Sankt-Jakobus Gesellschaft*, and so began the process of rediscovering the extensive network of jacobean pilgrimage routes originating in, or passing through, a still-divided Germany. This naturally led to scholarly enquiry into routes originating farther east. Meanwhile, in the United Kingdom, six English members of the French *Société des Amis* founded the *Confraternity of Saint James*. Among them were the well-known musicologist Dr. Mary Remnant, and Patricia Quaife, who would later carry out the investigation and lead the walks that revived Galicia's Camino Ingles.

Although these fledgling Associations were in touch with one another, the most vital communication for each of them at this early stage was with what we might call the 'centre of operations' in O Cebreiro here in Spain. An essential feature of this was the modest but now legendary *Boletín del Camino* produced every few months by

Don Elias. This consisted of a few typed and mimeographed pages, rolled and wrapped tightly with an address label by Don Elias and his family, sitting around the kitchen table of the Hospederia. Never was a table so much the centre of 'family life' as that table, since from it was sent forth the news and encouragement that kept the tiny jacobean 'family' of Europe informed and united! And it is also true, as I know through their personal testimonies, that those who helped in this task, sometimes by candlelight on winter evenings, never imagined that through their hands were passing the threads of a tapestry that one day would extend far beyond the destinations on those simple paper address slips, devised and typed out by Don Elias because they were cheaper than envelopes.

It wasn't long before a number of new Associations came into being, covering much of the European continent. These were usually started by a handful of people in each country who had made the pilgrimage to Santiago carrying the *Guía*, and returned home inspired. In the late 1980s there arose associations in Belgium and Holland, Portugal and Switzerland, and in the 90s, in Norway, Denmark, Austria and Ireland. In some countries where there is more than one official language, Associations have arisen to accommodate this fact, which is why there are two in Belgium and three in Switzerland. The panorama widened still further after the fall of the Berlin Wall in 1989. The revival of interest in the history of the pilgrimage in Eastern Europe, so long suppressed, was soon confirmed by the increasing numbers of pilgrims from Poland, the Czech Republic, Hungary, Slovakia, the former Baltic States and the separate countries that once comprised Yugoslavia.

More recently, in some countries such as the U.K. and France, and in Spain itself, there has been a move to form regional groups with the aim of supplying more detailed local information than that provided by the national Association, especially where there exists a traditional route and the cultural and monumental traces to justify its recuperation.

What have been the personal dynamics, the economic possibilities, that have brought these Associations into being? What services and activities do they offer to their audiences? The answers vary from country to country, not only because of the cultural differences arising from history, language or religion, but because good ideas need capable people to enact them, people with the ability to inspire others to share the work. With the benefit of first-hand knowledge, I can describe the experience of my own association, the Confraternity of St. James.

As an aside: I've noticed that it sometimes surprises continental European friends to learn that in the Middle Ages, England had a great devotion to the apostle James the Great, with more than 460 churches and chapels dedicated to him. This devotion was centred on a precious relic: the so-called 'Hand of St. James', brought there in the 12th century when Matilda, the daughter of king Henry I, returned home following the death of her husband, the Holy Roman Emperor. Henry I founded an abbey at Reading, some 70 kilometres west of London on the north bank of the Thames, to honour the relic and promote its veneration. For the next four centuries, Reading Abbey was a place of jacobean pilgrimage. Not even the Protestant reformation of the 16th century succeeded in wiping out devotion to St. James in England, though many churches were forced to alter their dedications, often to that of the Virgin Mary. Because of the reformers' opposition to the veneration of relics, many sanctuaries were destroyed, and Reading Abbey, with its cult of St James, was a major casualty.

I mention this historical background in order to make clear that when the Confraternity was founded, there was – as in other European countries - a historical context waiting to be revealed, a national heritage to be rediscovered. Across Europe, in response to the lead provided by Don Elias in his simple *Boletin*, the message of St. James and pilgrimage was taken up by the fledgling national Associations: a sense of the need -- the responsibility, even -- to revive an essential part of Europe's identity that had fallen into obscurity.

I can testify to this with reference to the aims of the Confraternity, set out at its first meeting on 13 January 1983. The six founder members agreed that their Association would be dedicated to the same purpose as the medieval jacobean confraternities: to assist in every possible way those who wished to make the pilgrimage to Compostela. This overarching purpose implied three constituent aims: to inform and educate the British public about the pilgrimage, to supply practical information to individual pilgrims, and to undertake research into the history of the pilgrimage in the British Isles. This last objective was seen as very necessary, since although the pilgrimage to Compostela was a well-documented and had left its traces everywhere in the country, it was still a subject little known or studied in academic circles.

The Confraternity's aims soon led to an ambitious programme. From its first few members, this demanded an immense amount of work, but also space in their homes and *ad hoc* financing that went on well into the 1990s. Its first year saw the creation of the *Bulletin* (initially four typed pages, today a substantial quarterly review, professionally printed); the first edition of the *Guide to the Camino Francés*, the establishment of its Library, and a cycle of cultural events, lectures and visits to places of jacobean interest. The first such visit was to the church of St Peter, Marlow, which possessed a relic alleged to be the once-famous hand of St James the Great, which had been recovered from the ruins of Reading Abbey in the 19th century. Before the Confraternity's first twelve months were out, the group of six members had grown to more than a hundred. The Spanish Ambassador to the United Kingdom, His Excellency Don José Puig de la Bellacasa, accepted the Confraternity's invitation to become its honorary President, and thus began a tradition followed by each of his successors.

In 1985, Belgium's biennial *Europalia* fair focused on Spain and its culture, and included a major exhibition on the place of the pilgrimage to Compostela in European history. The organisation of this event brought together experts from many fields (architecture, iconography, music and anthropology, to name a few) from all over the Continent, as well as scholars seeking to link their knowledge to the practical revival of the pilgrimage. The interest sparked by the exhibition not only boosted the membership of the Associations, but prompted numerous walkers and cyclists to re-enact the pilgrimage from their own front doors, with the aim of once again joining up local routes to the accepted feeder roads heading south-west to the Pyrenees.

The Confraternity had 200 members by the time the *Europalia* closed, and those inspired by what they had seen in Ghent became the mainstay of its study-tours to Santiago and other Camino cities. From 1986 through the 90s, Confraternity groups explored stretches of the French routes and areas of Spain. In the spring of 1986 there also took place in London the first 'Practical Pilgrim' day. These are now held in various parts of England and Scotland, with similar events organised by our sister associations in Ireland, Canada and the United States. These bring together experienced pilgrims and those who are preparing their journeys, for the exchange of information and the chance to look at maps and equipment.

The Confraternity Library and Slide Library were created through members' own contributions, and at the time of writing consist of a collection of 7,000 volumes and more than 3,000 slide images, open to the public for research and the preparation of talks, though borrowing is restricted to members. In the late 1980s and through the 1990s our members compiled a series of guidebooks to the jacobean routes in France and Spain. The audience for these is now international, the fact of being kept up to date (again, through the annotations provided by members), having made them the gold standard of pilgrim information. We also initiated a project to identify the vestiges of the pilgrimage in the United Kingdom, whether these were place-names, monuments such as churches or pilgrim hospitals, documentary references, or artistic creations such as images and stained glass, with the aim of producing a series of county guides to Britain's jacobean heritage.

I've given a brief overview of the activities begun by the Confraternity in its early years, on which we have continued to build, but in 1988 a new chapter opened. The Confraternity has always found ways for everyone to contribute, whatever their age or skills, but no project has brought out that particular quality more than our commitment to Refugio Gaucelmo, the pilgrim *albergue* in Rabanal del Camino, on the Camino Francés. How this project was conceived and realised is the subject for another occasion; I only want to mention here its importance to us as an Association. Our experience in Rabanal has shown us very clearly that offering our members a means of participating in the life of the Camino through 'giving something back' has become one of the most appreciated benefits of membership. It's gratifying to observe how, every spring before the refuge opens, a volunteer working party spends a week there painting and repairing. Hundreds of members have taken part in these, and the list of those wishing to volunteer is always full, months in advance. Their tasks aren't only the routine rectifying of wear and tear: members with the relevant skills have built dry-stone walls, repaired the tiled roofs, fashioned traditional timber doors, planted the herb garden, pruned the fruit trees and cleaned the chimneys.

This chance to 'give of themselves' has similarly prompted hundreds of others to train as wardens, or *hospitaleros*. Those who have served in that capacity in Rabanal come not only from the United Kingdom, but also from more than 20 other countries. I smile every time I hear someone call Refugio Gaucelmo 'the English albergue,' because it is probably the most truly international albergue on the entire Camino network.

The creation of Refugio Gaucelmo involved us in working closely with the diocese of Astorga and the *Amigos del Camino* based in Ponferrada, as well as with one another. This has tested and developed us as an Association, and forged what I call 'the spirit of the Confraternity', which underlies our attempt to make every pilgrim's stay the best it can be. This means that each and every pilgrim feels at home there. He or she is treated in a way that is not only consistent with the gospel message of charity, but with the age-old ethos of hospitality that is such a feature of the pilgrimage roads. When the pilgrim sets off again for Santiago, we do our best to ensure that it is with a sense of spiritual and physical renewal. In Camino tradition, pilgrims are invited to collaborate in the running of the refuge through a donation, but no-one has ever been turned away through lack of means, or even because they have declined to contribute.

To know that the Confraternity has become another link in the great chain of hospitality that sustained the Camino de Santiago through the centuries is profoundly moving. Moreover, we rejoice in the fact that Refugio Gaucelmo has been followed by other, similar ventures. I think especially of the albergue of San Nicolas de Puente Fitero, restored by Italy's *Confraternitá*, and the ones in Azofra and La Faba by the German cultural entity *Ultreia*. The German association *Sankt Christoforus Jugendswerk*, which aims at the social reinsertion of marginalised young people, has rehabilitated half a dozen albergues along the Camino Francés, including those at Hospital de Orbigo, Foncebadon and El Acebo.

It's not only the experience of traditional hospitality in the albergues, but contact with local people living along the route – their friendly welcome and random acts of kindness, their generosity, their patience with those who don't speak their language – that has the effect of opening pilgrims' hearts and minds. This is commonly cited by returned pilgrims, and I think may be more strongly felt by pilgrims from outside Spain. They are more deeply acquainted with the traveller's condition of vulnerability, having spent weeks or months on the road, far from home and familiar customs and native languages. The spark of basic human goodness, ignited by the way pilgrims are received day after day on the Camino, becomes the ember of gratitude from which the desire grows to 'go and do likewise' in the life to which they return.

Pilgrims who wish to maintain their connection with the Camino once they return home usually seek out their national or regional Association. Many of the continental groups have an advantage that the Confraternity does not: a dense network of recognised and documented medieval pilgrimage routes on their doorsteps. Sometimes the rediscovery and waymarking of former routes opens new horizons, not only for their members, but for pilgrims from neighbouring countries. An example of this comes from Germany, where for the past five years an international group of pilgrims has been waymarking the ancient route from Prague, via Tillyschanz and Nuremberg, to Konstanz on the Swiss border.

Another example is the call for collaboration in making the French route from Vézelay viable for walkers, through new waymarking and the organisation of modest infrastructure in the form of home-stays and gites. In Normandy, the ancient routes from the Channel that connect with larger ones leading to Paris and Poitiers are currently

St James the Great, from the portal of the basilica dedicated to him in Levoča, Slovakia. Many of Eastern Europe's historic pilgrim routes to Santiago have now been reclaimed and waymarked.
photo Miranda Jones

being recovered by a new Association. In Italy, an organisation linked to the Council of Europe is promoting the Via Francigena, ensuring that once again, that venerable road is carrying pilgrims from north of the Alps to Rome, as well as those walking in the opposite direction, from Rome to Santiago. And in Norway, through the efforts of its jacobean Association, the medieval pilgrimage from Oslo to the shrine of St Olav at Nidaros is once again being enacted along the newly waymarked footpath, some 700 kilometres long.

As the great German writer Johann Wolfgang von Goethe put it in the eighteenth century, "Europe was made on the pilgrim road to Compostela." This memorable phrase means that in the Middle Ages, many of the culturally defining features of a specifically European outlook and awareness were carried by pilgrims who came to Santiago from every corner of the known world, and carried back home when their pilgrimages were over. These features included the romanesque and gothic architectural styles, troubadour poetry, music of every kind and the instruments to play it on, discoveries in medicine and the natural sciences, plant breeding, viticulture and gastronomy, the legends and miracles of the saints, and words and expressions borrowed from one language and introduced into another.

Medieval pilgrims set out impelled by faith, and most probably returned home with their faith strengthened. As the late Professor William Melczer wrote, "the medieval pilgrims to the tomb of the apostle could not have completed the enormous distances from Central Europe to Compostela and back, had they not already been carrying Santiago in their hearts." In today's secular society, it's doubtful whether this is true in all cases. We can say with certainty that it continues to be so in many.

What we can affirm, more generally, is that pilgrims return home with a new confidence, not only in themselves, but also in a world inhabited by people who are both similar to and different from themselves. Many will take to the road again. Most will tell of their experience and inspire others. The facilitating link between one journey and the next, one pilgrim and the next, is the Association, that group of passionately committed supporters, often themselves Camino veterans, whose help is vital both in preparing pilgrims and receiving them home again. They are the heralds of the pilgrimage in our time, with its joyful affirmation of values beyond those of the marketplace, which sometimes seem so dominant. They are also its guardians, conserving a European identity that flourishes organically from its spiritual and cultural roots.

In closing, I am moved to express my appreciation to you, the residents of Santiago, for the marvellous welcome that you continue to give, year after year, to the pilgrims of Europe and the world. It joins the memories of the Camino in accompanying them on their journeys home, where tomorrow their pilgrimages begin.

8

The Way of Saint James: some European Models of the Praxis of Transformation. Presented at the VII International Conference of Jacobean Associations *El Camino de Santiago, Puente Hacia una Nueva Europa* (The Way of Saint James, a Bridge Towards a New Europe), Ponferrada, 20-23 October 2005.

Although I am not personally associated with any of the organisations I will discuss today, their work over the years has earned my respect, and makes me want to make them better known. Even on the Camino de Santiago, which is so central to their activities, they are not as well recognised as they deserve to be. Why is that the case? First, because all three are based abroad: in Belgium, Germany and France. And secondly, because they work unobtrusively, without calling attention to themselves. None the less, "by their fruits" each makes a valuable contribution to the inclusive and renovative character of the Camino de Santiago, and to society at large.*

What is the meaning of this word 'praxis?' What has it to do with 'transformation', the other term we use so often in speaking of the Camino de Santiago? The Oxford English Dictionary defines the Greek word 'praxis' simply as 'the use of a theory or a belief in a practical way'. Great religions and philosophies are united in teaching that words and feelings are insufficient when confronting the world's problems. If we believe in a religion, a philosophy or a political system, the commitment to live according to our belief demands expression. Does 'praxis', then, simply mean 'to take the practical action that is consistent with what we believe in'?

I don't think we can properly speak of 'praxis' in relation to evil. It can only be applied to acts undertaken with good intentions, through the exercise of our free will. And we do not engage in 'praxis' when we seek 'the good' solely for our own benefit; 'praxis' should properly have as its primary objective the good of others. Therefore, returning to the title of this paper, the 'praxis of transformation' is the practical action, taken altruistically according to one's convictions, that makes it possible for someone or something to be transformed, to experience change for the better. It presupposes that the person acting has already experienced something of the good being sought for another. The aim is to offer that 'other' the *possibility of transformation* - in other words, to provide him or her with the external circumstances through which interior change may be possible.

The first organisation I'd like to describe is *Oikoten* of Belgium, which since 1982 has sought alternatives to the social exclusion of young delinquents and disadvantaged minors. The philosophy of Oikoten is based on an 'emancipatory pedagogy' in which adolescents with severe social problems are helped, not by shielding them, but by treating them as adults and giving them real responsibilities. The original founders were moved by the situations of young people for whom traditional institutions seemed to offer no solutions. Institutional life, lack of education, socially unacceptable behaviour and criminality seemed likely prescriptions for future failure.

'*Oikoten*' is another Greek word. It means both 'far from home' and 'by your own efforts or means'. Over the years it has also acquired, according to the organisation itself, the meaning of 'to pull up by the roots' and replant in another place. The name perfectly encapsulates the intention and effects of the journeys on foot over great distances that constitute its basic activity. *Oikoten* follows an important historical precedent, originating in the Low Countries in the Middle Ages. This was the custom of juridically imposing pilgrimages to Santiago de Compostela as criminal sentences. Once accomplished, the journey allowed the 'pilgrims' to regain their freedom without further punishment.

The first Oikoten journey took place in 1982. Two delinquent minors from a government institution, accompanied by a monitor, walked from Vézelay in France to Santiago, a distance of 2,500 kilometres. They carried everything in rucksacks, and slept in tents. In principle, it seemed unlikely the expedition would be a success: the psychological stability of the boys could not be counted on, and they were a security risk, with a propensity for escape. But contrary to some predictions, the three arrived safe and sound in Santiago after a four-month trek. Later, the two minors were able to rejoin mainstream society.

This first journey was the prototype for more projects in the years that followed. Girls were included from 1987. The number of projects has increased to include journeys on other routes – on one occasion, by bicycle from Algeria up the Via de la Plata to Santiago. Other youths made lengthy trips through India, Africa and Eastern Europe. (Oikoten also generated a further important initiative in 1987: a mediation service between violent young offenders and their victims, but this unfortunately lies outside the scope of this presentation.) The idea behind all these activities was the same: to transplant a young person 'by the roots' from an environment that fosters only negative tendencies, to new surroundings that require the discovery and development of inner resources and abilities.

Oikoten clients have led turbulent lives. Many live for years in custodial institutions; others come from broken families and are traumatised by violence or sexual abuse. Almost all suffer from low self-esteem, and for many, the conviction that no one loves them causes depression. In others, this lack of emotional attachment leads them to manipulate others, steal, and lie. Relations with their parents, schools and institutions are riddled with conflict, to the point where some of these minors are viewed as impossible to control, even incorrigible.

To remove them from their habitual ambience and put them in another in which they are challenged to assume a role with radically different social expectations – for example, 'I am a pilgrim to Santiago' instead of 'I am a juvenile delinquent' – has the effect of helping the young person to acquire another definition and vision of himself, another sense of identity. How is this achieved? By spending several months walking in the open air, living a healthy and simple life with the support and supervision of a guide *in loco parentis*, a professional who has the gift of communicating with troubled young people. The young person's companions have equally problematical backgrounds, and each young offender must learn to get along with others. Each must assume a share of responsibility for the communal life of the group: putting up the tents, doing the shopping, managing the money... even learning to follow a recipe when it is his or her turn to cook.

The rhythm of the day demands great physical effort. Walking for several hours each day gives the young people time for reflection. Together, they learn to do useful things, and out of their shared experiences emerge the first stirrings of solidarity. There is free time, and they must decide what to do with it: they are 'free' to commit anti-social acts, or to take measures to avoid committing them. Conquering the day's obstacles – geographical, physical, personal – promotes self-confidence. They are surprised, as all pilgrims are, to meet people living along the route who react positively to them, who encourage them with a kind word, or who give them things – fruit from a garden tree, for instance - without expecting anything more than a 'thank you' in return. Little by little, the hard and negative perceptions of these young people are replaced by a more balanced view of the world, and new perspectives open. By the time they reach Santiago, each feels that he or she has accomplished something worthy of respect. They are proud of being physically fit. They've enjoyed living a 'normal' life in the preceding months – enough to see it as a real alternative to the way they lived before.

A project in which young people are 'pulled up by the roots' requires detailed administrative and practical groundwork. In the view of the juvenile court judge, the project must offer a genuine alternative to a custodial sentence, and new perspectives not likely to be achieved by other means. The offender permitted to take part in an Oikoten project must be over 16, and write a letter demonstrating adequate motivation and commitment. Those addicted to drugs or alcohol cannot be considered. The young person signs a contract that sets out four rules: 1) to walk every step of the way 2) to respect the law 3) to leave portable music devices and mobile phones behind, and 4) to avoid behaviour that could endanger the expedition.

Each project has at least one Oikoten staff member, or monitor, depending on the size of the group, who act as guides, plus a personal supporter back in Belgium for each participant. These 'supporters' act as intermediaries: they receive the letters written while the participants are on the move; they maintain contact with parents and the legal system, and prepare the celebratory homecoming. Before leaving, the young people spend a few days at the Oikoten headquarters, absorbing the ethos of the trip and getting into shape by walking each day. The night before departure, the contracts are signed by each young person, his family, his guide, supporters, and an Oikoten official. This ceremony demonstrates that the trip is being taken seriously by everyone, and reminds participants that their responsibility is collective as well as individual.

And what is the effect, in personal and social terms, of the Oikoten projects? It is impossible to summarise the dozens of projects that have changed the lives of hundreds of adolescents over a period of more than twenty years. Two studies carried out in 1992 and 1994 by Oikoten and the University of Louvain demonstrated that up until then, more than 60% of Oikoten participants reintegrated well into society, while the other 40% continued to have difficulties. Keeping in mind the poor prospects for these young people before their journeys, these results suggest the trips have a strongly beneficial effect. (In England, the percentages of young offenders who reintegrate and reoffend are almost the inverse of the Oikoten figures. As one official from the Felsted reformatory just outside London told me, only 30% of the young offenders released in a given year succeed in re-entering society; within three years, the other 70% are once again in custody.)

Although it is hard to make a general correlation between an Oikoten journey and the subsequent personal histories of those who have taken part, many of the young people themselves, in their own words, have been convinced that walking to Santiago has shown them another way forward. Their newly gained self-confidence has fostered the willingness to accept responsibility, and the ability to persevere in achieving their goals. Bitterness has given way to healthy ambitions, such as qualifying in some trade or profession, or buying a flat, and to an improvement in relations with their parents and the authorities. For many, the positive influence extends to every area of their lives. In fact, what they are describing is personal transformation.

I now invite you to take a look at another organisation that works with young people who are seriously disadvantaged. This is the *Christophorus Jugendwerk Oberimsingen*, based in Freiburg, Germany. Its field is supplementary and remedial education, and its mission is 'to work with young people who have failed in every other area of assistance' and who, like those of Oikoten, '...come from the jails, the psychiatric centres, and life on the streets'. The

Christophorus Jugendwerk, as an institution linked to the Catholic humanitarian organisation *Caritas*, sees its task as pastoral, implying the transmission of Christian values. Usually the young people, aged 16 or 17, to whom it extends a hand have had hardly any contact with the Church: some have never been inside a church building, and have never heard a prayer.

These young people are at a stage in which they are trying to discover and build their own identities, and are more open to fresh experiences than one might think. Thus, in 1991, there arose the idea within the Christophorus Jugendwerk of taking some of these teenagers along the Camino de Santiago to experience its beneficial effects. As the organisation itself says in one of its documents,

Mankind through the centuries has used the impressions and experiences lived on the Camino de Santiago to answer the great questions of life, to learn their own limits – to accept them and go beyond them – so as to understand the ultimate meaning of existence and of their own selves.... All these experiences we would like also to make available to these young people.

The Christophorus Jugendwerk believed from the outset that these pilgrimage journeys should be linked to practical projects. Supported financially by Daimler-Benz of Stuttgart, with the participation of the *Deutsche Sankt Jakobus Gesellschaft* in Germany, the Pallotine Fathers in Spain, and that great humanitarian and friend of the Camino, the late Dr. Herbert Simon, groups of young people from both countries worked together over three summers between 1991 and 1993 to build a pilgrims' *albergue* in the parish house at Hospital de Orbigo. Between 1994 and 1997, other groups did the same in the parish house at Santibañez de Valdeiglesias. Between 1998 and 2000, the ruined church at Foncebadón was rebuilt as an *albergue*. More than 100 adolescents from the Christophorus Jugendwerk took part in these construction projects, working side by side with young people from the diocese of Astorga.

The aim of the Christophorus Jugendwerk is the social reintegration of young people, both those who are already in trouble and those at serious risk. It tries to give them 'perspectives, and the development and maintenance of solid values in the form of social skills and... the completion of their schooling and professional training'. On the Camino de Santiago, which it calls 'a way of encounter' it has created situations in which the energies of these young people, which might otherwise lead them astray, can be channelled and expressed in projects that are beneficial both to themselves and to other pilgrims. I quote once again the words of its Director General, Norbert Scheiwe: on the Camino, he affirms, 'The youngsters live in another context, exceeding their own expectations, and, on an international level, demanding of themselves and growing into themselves, leaving aside their unhappy past lives and looking ahead towards the future that awaits them'.

The third entity to which I want to draw your attention is the community known as the *Hospitalité Saint Jacques*, which has found a home in the French village of Estaing, a day's walk before Conques on the Le Puy route. Here we have one of the most remarkable initiatives in the whole network of routes leading to the tomb of St James. It began with a married couple and the wife's brother, who made their pilgrimage to Santiago in 1990. On returning to their homes and jobs in the north of France, each of the three felt a strong call to serve other pilgrims by forming a lay Christian community, where pilgrims could be welcomed and spiritually accompanied on their journeys. A year later, they resigned their jobs, sold their homes and belongings, and left the north behind. They travelled to Le Puy and on to Aveyron, where, in the diocese of Rodez, they met a bishop who understood their mission. He offered them a house in Estaing where they could receive pilgrims and the poor in the spirit of the Gospels. The three founders opened the house to pilgrims in 1992. Since then, with the addition of another family, they have lived out their founding mission quietly, but with undoubted influence.

A few years ago, members of the Confraternity had the good fortune to hear a talk given by a member of the community, whom we had invited to attend our second international conference, on the theme of 'hospitality'. I don't think I can do better than to quote her, in trying to describe the Hospitalité Saint Jacques's mission to pilgrims. She described how:

'The community lives through prayer, for the task of offering welcome, of evangelisation, and for anything that God may ask of us for the benefit of all. It is a link in a chain of places of Christian welcome – parishes, families, convents and monasteries – to which it imparts its own particular stamp. Together with the Premonstratensian community of Conques, we seek to be part of this chain by setting out a statement of welcome with four points. We want to show pilgrims to Santiago something of the Christian spirit of welcome, as a counterweight to secularisation and commercialisation. The four points are: 1) to make ourselves available 2) to pray with pilgrims, or to put at their disposal a place of prayer 3) to commit ourselves to praying for pilgrims, and 4) to offer them a free choice in contributing to the cost of their stay.'

In explaining how the work of receiving pilgrims is regarded, she said:

'Pilgrims are a reflection of humankind, with their interior riches, their deep longings and anxieties. Our daily task is to receive this humanity – walking, searching – and offer it to God. The daily expression of our faith is to recognise in each pilgrim the presence of Christ Himself. In this double action it is hard to know who gives and who receives (remember that in French the same word means both 'host' and 'guest'). We have to live this as a constant exchange. What we offer to the existential fragility of a pilgrim – a roof, a few comforts, a gathering in an atmosphere of peace and prayer – is repaid a hundred times over, in both the material sense and in the countless ways of the Spirit, which cannot be quantified. We would happily give everything for the privilege of welcoming Jesus every day! This mission of welcome, then, is a privilege, a grace. It has transformed our lives and we hope it will continue to transform them.'

The community is firm in its vision of the Camino as a route of faith, of prayer and asceticism, in which the task of the pilgrim is to clothe himself with the spirit of pilgrimage, and the task of a place of welcome such as their own is to help their fellow-pilgrims to come closer to an encounter with God and with the mystery of Providence. Therefore – and I quote again – 'places of welcome cannot be spiritually neutral' without betraying the essential nature of the pilgrimage.

These specifically Christian places of welcome maintain the most authentic jacobean tradition, but at the same time they derive their legitimacy from a profound respect for the spiritual freedom of every pilgrim. The community affirms roundly, as did the abbot of Roncesvalles in the 13th century, that 'the door is open to all – to the sick and the well, not only to Catholics but to pagans, Jews, heretics, the shiftless and the vagabonds, the well-heeled and the worldly' – in other words, to everyone who walks the Camino, without distinction.

If to receive pilgrims, as to receive the poor and the unhappy, is a work of mercy, then offering welcome becomes an apostolate. It is free because there is no price you can put on it (or, in the striking question put to us by our speaker, 'How much would you charge Christ if He were your guest?'). This is not because the expenses do not mount up, but because they are secondary to what, first and foremost, the community offers the pilgrim: the acknowledgment of brotherhood in Christ, their trust, their availability, their patience... one might as well say 'themselves'. The way the house is furnished (dignified and clean, but simply), reflects the joy of being together in the presence of God, without the need for luxuries or over-decoration.

At the Hospitalité Saint Jacques, the presence of God in the pilgrim is respected, but it is also offered to him: through the sacraments when possible, and through the community's prayer, in which the pilgrim is invited to take part. The community celebrates the Liturgy of the Hours. After Lauds each morning it expresses its mission to accompany pilgrims by reading aloud the names of all who have passed through in the previous two months – the time estimated to reach Compostela. (This is a practice that has spread to other places on the Caminos, as many of us will know.) Within the rhythm of the day established by prayer, the community tries to maintain a simple and peaceful family atmosphere. It is this atmosphere that it seeks to transmit to pilgrims when they cross the threshold. The house is not just a collection of facilities to which the pilgrim has access; it is literally *his or her home* while staying there, in which everything facilitates the restoration of physical strength and the nourishment of the soul. The community depends entirely upon Providence for its economic survival: as our speaker told us, 'the Holy Spirit will inspire the generosity needed for His work to continue'.

What does it mean for a pilgrim to become part of the Hospitalité Saint Jacques, even for a day or two? My colleague Dr William Griffiths, who currently chairs the Confraternity of Saint James, has told me some of his own reactions (and I quote):

"I like to think of pilgrimage as the insulation around a live electric wire: no human being can bear the direct experience of God, and so we "insulate" it with layers of art, history, culture and companionship.... Every now and then we meet people on the Camino who penetrate the insulation and reveal that they understand why we are pilgrims. I and a companion had such an experience at Estaing in 1993. We were made welcome, and allowed to stay a few days to rest and share the life of the community, and especially the prayer that is at the heart of it. We saw how the community prays daily for pilgrims, we saw the warm welcome given to tramps ('our fellow wayfarers'). Before leaving, I already knew I wanted to return as a *hospitalero* – something I have done in most years since then. I came to understand the community better – its total dependence on divine Providence, the happiness its members feel when St James or one of its other patron saints works a small miracle, and the delicate balance between family life and the life of the community, in which a varying number of pilgrims each day are included. I observed how, with infinite tact, they offered pilgrims the chance to deepen the spiritual meaning of their journeys. I also noted their concern, similarly delicate and unobtrusive, that *hospitaleros* become aware of the privilege they were being granted of welcoming Christ in the person of the pilgrim."

The Hospitalité Saint Jacques exists because of, and for, the Camino de Santiago. Like many jacobean associations, it is challenged by the secularisation of society in general, and by massification on the Camino. In order to remain open to everyone, many places offering hospitality have had to downplay the importance of the sanctuary in Galicia as a place of grace, in favour of an emphasis on the Camino itself, and the provision of information about 'how to do it'. The Hospitalité respectfully affirms that conventional piety is not enough. Its mission is to pray and to serve.

'We have to be witnesses at every moment to the love of Christ without holding back, in order to offer a response, in the spirit of the pilgrimage, to the spiritual thirst felt by so many people today,' our speaker told us. And in a phrase which strikes me as exceptionally beautiful, she affirmed that 'No one is forced to drink, but it is asked of us that we offer the water'.

I recall again the three organisations discussed: Oikoten, the Christophorus Jugendwerk, and the Hospitalité Saint Jacques. Each is composed of people who give of themselves, who are committed in different ways to transmitting to others what they themselves have received from their experience as pilgrims on the Camino. There are various observations that emerge from a consideration of their work.

All of their labours emphasise the Camino's inclusivity. The figure of *homo viator* has almost become a cliché when speaking of the Camino, but like most such expressions, it contains an essential truth. The Camino is for everyone, precisely because the journey along it is a metaphor for life itself. We are all on the Camino, pilgrims making our way along the road marked out by the chronological stages between birth and death. In this sense, no-one is left out, whatever his or her social or economic condition. Neither the advantages nor the disadvantages of life absolve us from the responsibility of making of ourselves, in our brief journeys, the best 'selves' we can. As the 'way of encounter' and the school of the virtues that it is, the Camino presents us with fresh, new experiences every day, and at the same time, it invites us to improve the way we receive them. Like life itself, but more intensely, the Camino invites us to grow in every moment, 'by walking, to make the road' as Antonio Machado's famous phrase puts it. Life is a road that inwardly impels us onward, a mystery that is only resolved, one step at a time, through *praxis*.

This gives hope to many, but especially to the young people of Oikoten and the Christophorus Jugendwerk, who, through circumstance, need help in putting themselves on this geographical and metaphorical 'Camino'. It allows them – forces them! – to live each day as if it were the first, to begin again, to cease to be defined by their past. It shows them it is not too late to rectify harm done, to be changed from within, to carry on with their lives in another frame of reference. Some would call this awakening to the fullness of life, to the beauty of nature, to the respect and companionship the Camino offers them 'wisdom'. I would call it 'grace'. Call it what you will, it is something that cannot spring up in the heart until a person feels valued and loved for himself alone. This applies equally to the pilgrim who passes through the open door of the Hospitalité Saint Jacques, as to the adolescent for whom the Camino may be his last opportunity.

Our three organisations show us, as they seek to show those they work with, that a necessary quality for being on the 'camino of encounter' is the openness that allows it to change us from within. (Paradoxically, this attitude may be easier to communicate to a young person who has nothing to lose, than to a pilgrim who wants an 'easy' Camino, isolating himself from others by sleeping in hotels and being permanently connected to a mobile phone!) This is a radical change to a vision of the world, one that recognises not just a person's social or economic status, but his or her character; and the true value of material things – not their brand-names and prices, but their usefulness in the task of living coherently what has been learned. These are prerequisites for speaking with conviction about the Camino. We cannot pass on what we do not have in the first place.

And finally, I would like to refer to that comment about the mission of the Hospitalité Saint Jacques. 'Who gives, and who receives?' when the door is opened and the *hospitalero* sees, in the figure of the exhausted pilgrim, the person of Christ Himself? The *hospitalero* - and whoever has been granted, among the gifts of his Camino, the understanding that every person is a brother or a sister - sees the arrival of the pilgrim as a blessing. He recognises not only Christ, but also, in a sense, himself. He recalls how he, as a pilgrim, felt when a door opened and someone welcomed him. Those who are active in Oikoten and the Christophorus Jugendwerk also see

FR. ANGEL FERNÁNDEZ DE ARÁNGUIZ, S.A.C., BROUGHT TOGETHER THE CHRISTOPHORUS JUGENDWERK AND YOUNG PEOPLE FROM THE PROVINCES OF ASTORGA AND LEON TO CREATE NINE ALBERGUES ON THE CAMINO FRANCES.

PHOTO *PEREGRINO*

the potential inherent in their young charges: the people they could become, if their circumstances can be altered. To alter them, on their behalf, is to engage in the praxis of transformation. In becoming the agent of praxis, the person who acts is also changed; *he or she receives, and in receiving, is transformed*. The great Spanish writer Miguel de Unamuno expressed it as follows:

> *"I give what I have," says the generous soul.*
> *"I give all I can," says the one moved by self-denial.*
> *"I give what I am," says the hero.*
> *"In giving of myself, I am blessed to receive," says the saint.*

(*)As of 2022 the Christophorus Jugendwerk continues its mission. The Hospitalité Saint Jacques is closed indefinitely due to illness. Oikoten has been absorbed into other organizations that are part of the Belgian juvenile justice system. Its founder, Willi Derveaux, was honored in January 2023 with a portrait bust outside Albergue Ave Fenix in Villafranca de Bierzo."

9

The Origins Of Holy Years And The *Compostela*. A Paper given at a study-weekend on 'Holy Years and Souvenirs' organized by the Confraternity of Saint James at The Friars, Aylesford Priory, Kent, 26-28 February 1999. It was published in Bulletin 65 (March 2000) and later, together with Patricia Quaife's 'Holy Year Curiosities', as Confraternity Occasional Paper 7.

The terms 'Holy Year' and 'Año Santo', 'Año Jacobeo' or 'Xacobeo', 'Jubilee' and 'Jubilee Indulgence', 'credencial' and 'compostela' are ones we have probably heard very often since we have had anything to do with the Confraternity and the pilgrimage to Santiago. Given how often we encounter them, it seemed to me that it might be both useful and interesting to investigate their origins and meanings in today's Study Day. I propose in this talk to consider, firstly, the history of the important concept of the 'jubilee' and the idea of generalised pardon, both of which are often included in the term 'holy year', and secondly, the history of that document so closely associated with the pilgrimage to Santiago, the *compostela.*

In discussing the origins of jubilees and holy years, I need to refer briefly to a further idea, that of the 'sabbatical', which we will also recognise as a modern survival. The concept of a time of remission in which land and people were returned to their original state is a very ancient one. In the Judeo-Christian tradition, it is found in the Mosaic Law. During the Israelites' years in the wilderness, the alienation of family goods and the development of money-lending at interest had as a consequence an increase in poverty and indebtedness. This was contrary to the social equality that had existed during the confederacy of the tribes of Israel, and which was still an ideal in the time of Moses. To redress this undesirable development, as the Pentateuch relates, the sabbatical year and the jubilee year were instituted.

The cycle of years that ended with one in which the land was allowed to lie fallow was modeled on the creation cycle ending in a day of rest. But the 'sabbatical' year included additional social components. Chapters 21 to 23 of the Book of Exodus specify that slaves were to be given their liberty after seven years, and that every seven years, the produce of the vine and the olive were to be left unharvested for the benefit of the poor. Deuteronomy, chapter 15, institutes the 'remission', or *semittah,* which provides for the return, every seventh year, of goods held in satisfaction of personal debts. In Leviticus, chapter 25, we again find the provision of a cyclic period of repose for the land. Historical references dating from later periods suggest that in practice the sabbatical year may have been difficult to effect: the First Book of Maccabees, chapter 6, tells us that the Jews were short of provisions "because it was a sabbatical year conceded to the earth". In the reign of Herod the Great, the revered rabbi Hillel was the originator of a clause in contracts whereby the signatories agreed to forego the privileges of remission, liberty, *et cetera*, given to them by the sabbatical year - presumably because the cost of granting them was prohibitive.

The sabbatical, then, was an ancient institution, but it is hard to gauge how faithfully it was observed. It did, nonetheless, underlie the concept of the Jubilee year, which, as Leviticus, (chapter 25, verse 10) proclaimed, was a year of rest and remission that was to take place every fifty years - that is, as the culmination of a cycle of seven sabbaticals: 'You will declare holy the fiftieth year, and you will proclaim in the land the liberty of all the inhabitants: this will be for you a jubilee'. The etymology of the word 'jubilee' lies in the latin *jubilæus*, from the Hebrew *yóbel*, the word for the horn that was blown to announce the start of the year. The jubilee was a full-scale exemption from prevailing economic conditions for the entire population. As in the sabbatical, the land was to lie uncultivated, property was to revert to its original owner, and insolvent debtors were to be released. In practice, again, this would have been a difficult law to enforce and to fulfil. Coming immediately after the seventh sabbatical year, the jubilee would have meant *two* fallow years, two years in succession when many habitual transactions were suspended. The law of the jubilee is very unlikely ever to have been practiced and seems to have proposed an ideal of justice and social equality that was longed for, but never achieved. It implied a revolution in social and economic life, as the prelude to spiritual conversion, a turning away from the affairs of the world to render due homage to God (1).

It is in this sense that the idea of the jubilee found its way into Christian thought. St. John's Gospel speaks of the power of Christ's teaching to liberate from the tyranny of sin. Isidore of Seville absorbed the linking of this teaching with the idea of the jubilee from the writings of St Jerome, and in his *Etymologies* (V, 37, iii) clearly defined the jubilee year as 'a year of remission of sins'. In the Latin translations of the psalms, words with the same root but the somewhat different meaning of 'shouts' or 'popular cries' were used to express the joyful acclaim of a people whose God was all-powerful: 'jubilation' as a natural component of the call to conversion.

To carry all this forward to the early 12th century, and link it to the pilgrimage to Compostela, it is necessary to say something about the doctrine of indulgences. The heightened awareness of sin and death that seems to us so characteristic of the medieval mind was counterbalanced by the promise offered by this doctrine. According to it, all sin, short of actual mortal sin that entails the eternal punishment of separation from God, requires satisfaction, either here on earth or after death, in the purifying state called Purgatory. Sins can be absolved on earth, but the so-called 'temporal punishment' for them remains, in this time of purification after death. Very simply, an indulgence is a remission of the temporal punishment due for sin (2). Obtaining them is thus a way of reducing the time spent after death in Purgatory. The first indulgences were general and partial, remitting a quarter or half of the penalty for the faithful who satisfied conditions such as going on pilgrimage and almsgiving. By the mid-11th century, the Church was promising particularly generous indulgences to those participating in the reconquest of Spain, or making especially long and arduous journeys to the shrines of the saints.

There is more to be said about indulgences a little farther on, but for the moment let us shift our attention to the city of Compostela at the beginning of the 12th century. By then pilgrims had been making their way to the shrine of St James, mainly from France and central Europe, in increasing numbers - although we do not know precisely how many - for more than a century. This is not the place to review the many interconnected reasons for the growing fame of the Apostle's tomb up to this time, nor for an overview of the pilgrimage phenomenon, with its variety of motives and its important areas of enquiry such as the veneration of relics. Rather, we will simply remind ourselves that the pilgrimage to the shrine of St James the Great, the 'first among the Apostles' to gain the crown of martyrdom, was by now well-established. After the destruction of the first modest church honouring him, a somewhat grander one had been built. As the saint's reputation for miracles spread, a magnificent new basilica had arisen around this church. With the translation of the former see of Iria Flavia to Compostela in 1095, this splendid creation became a cathedral.

In the year 1100 the dynamic and cosmopolitan Diego Gelmírez became Bishop of Compostela (3). In the course of his 40-year episcopate, he would succeed in raising the stature of his already renowned see to rival that of Rome itself. Initially, this was not easy:

the Roman curia had apparently regarded Compostela with hostility ever since a papal legate was given a chilly reception there in 1068, and the growing pilgrimage to the shrine of St James, together with the pretensions and wealth of the cathedral, fed the idea that this far-off Iberian bishopric was a potential, if not an actual, rival. Gelmírez, however, was a consummate politician, and undertook to align himself with Rome for the furtherance of his diocese. Four years after assuming office he was made an archbishop by Pope Pascual II. In 1109 the same pope allowed him the privilege of designating seven of his canons 'cardinals' who were to celebrate mass at the high altar, and for the great religious feasts, adorn themselves with mitres as Roman cardinals did. Curial suspicions were allayed, and interest in the prosperity of the compostellan cathedral assured, by making Roman cardinals canons of the latter. The intention was no doubt to deflect attention from the fact that the shrine of St James was almost as much visited by pilgrims as that of St Peter.

Gelmírez's ambitions were further realised with the accession to the papacy in 1119 of Guy of Burgundy (son of the count of Burgundy and formerly bishop of the French see of Vienne) who took the papal name of Calixtus II. Guy's brother Raymond had become count of Galicia on his marriage to Doña Urraca, the daughter of Alfonso VI, and at one time Gelmírez had served as Raymond's chancellor. Pope Calixtus II was thus the uncle of the young Alfonso VII, king of Castile, Leon and Galicia; he was well acquainted with Archbishop Gelmírez, and viewed favourably his efforts to promote the see of Compostela. The name of Calixtus II would become, through the dedication to him of the famous *Liber Sancti Jacobi*, among other reasons, one of the most important in the history of the pilgrimage. In 1120 he granted the see of Compostela the metropolitan status - that is, authority over a given area - hitherto held by the ancient see of Mérida, and made Gelmírez papal legate in the sees of Mérida and Braga.

Ever since 1095 and Pope Urban II's proclamation of the First Crusade, those who went on pilgrimage to the Holy Land had been promised a plenary indulgence - that full remission of the temporal punishment for sin mentioned earlier - if they died on their journey. This established a link between pilgrimage and plenary indulgences that, as travel to the Holy Land became more fraught with danger and the pilgrimage to Compostela was promoted and protected, became an important motivation among pilgrims undertaking the Way of St James. Contrary to the manner in which it is often presented, however, the truth about the documented beginnings of this association is far from clear (4). It is often claimed (in the popular publications issuing from the cathedral in Santiago) that Pope Calixtus gave to Compostela, in 1122, the privilege of granting a plenary indulgence to the faithful who visited the shrine of the Apostle, availed themselves of the sacrament of confession, attended Mass, gave a donation for the upkeep of the shrine, and performed good works during each year when the feast of St James, 25 July, fell on a Sunday. This privilege is confidently declared to have been confirmed by Calixtus's successors before being made perpetual in 1179 by Pope Alexander III by means of the bull *Regis Aeterni.* It is on a later copy of this document that Compostela rests its claim that 'jubilees' have taken place since 1122, in a recurring and unbroken pattern of 6, 5, 6 and 11 years. The "jubilee' is both the year in which a plenary indulgence can be gained, and the indulgence itself, hence the phrase 'to gain the jubilee' ("ganar el jubileo") which one so often hears in Spain. (It is important to remember that any baptised person coming to the shrine in a Holy Year, with the right interior dispositions and carrying out the designated acts of piety, can obtain the jubilee indulgence. In any Holy Year, thousands of people from Santiago itself also 'gain the jubilee' without walking more than a few hundred metres.)

About the authenticity of the bull *Regis Aeterni,* however, there has been grave doubt since the end of the nineteenth century and the publication of the *Historia de la S.A.M. Iglesia de Santiago de Compostela,* a vast 11 volume work by the compostellan cathedral historian and archivist, A. López Ferreiro. According to him, and to later scholars, the surviving copy of Alexander III's bull contains linguistic and other anachronisms which rule out a 12th century date (5). It is indeed strange, given that it was only in the year 1300 that Pope Boniface VIII instituted the Roman jubilee that was to take place every 50 years, to find in the purported Alexandrine bull of 121 years earlier the declaration that the jubilee indulgences obtained by the faithful at the shrine of St James be 'gained in the same way and manner as in the Roman Church'.

The earliest documented account of the indulgences granted to jacobean pilgrims by the various popes in fact dates only from the mid-13th century, forming part of the proceedings of a compostellan diocesan council (6). There is no indication of when each of the indulgences was conceded, nor by which individual pope. Neither is anything said about a particular privilege related to years when the saint's feast-day fell on a Sunday. Of the indulgences mentioned, the only plenary one is to pilgrims who died during their journey; the others were partial: 40 days' remission for taking part in the Sunday procession; 240 days for attending a mass celebrated by the compostellan archbishop or cardinals (that is, at the high altar); 200 days for attending a mass celebrated at the altar of St James; 600 days and remission of one-third of one's temporal punishment for keeping the saint's vigil and feast, and the feast of the dedication of cathedral, (21 April); and one-third for having made the pilgrimage at all. It is possible, though not proven, that Calixtus II may have granted some of these, and that Innocent III may have granted the one relating to the dedication of the cathedral for the dedication celebration of 1211. Whatever their origin, these indulgences were still in force, with some modifications, at the end of the 15th century. Samuel Purchas's anonymous English pilgrim jotted them down in 1422, and William Wey in 1456.

Although the existing copy of *Regis Aeterni* is accepted by most modem scholars as a forgery, there is disagreement over its possible date. Could it, for instance, have been compiled not too long after the celebration of the second Roman Jubilee in 1350 – perhaps by a highly-placed cleric who had seen at first hand the dynamic effect the celebration had produced in the number of pilgrims visiting Rome, and who wished to stem the decline in the numbers making their way to Compostela during a time of plague and intermittent war? Most often, the document is attributed either to the early or late 14th century. (Nonetheless, we still see it tacitly accepted on every side that compostellan jubilees have been celebrated since 1122). Giving some support to a later 14th century date for *Regis Aeterni*, Constance Storrs' earliest indentifiable jubilee year, on the basis of a great increase in the number of licenses to ships carrying pilgrims, is 1395; her next is 1417 (although 25 July also fell on Sunday in 1400 and 1406) (7). Fernando López Alsina suggests that plenary indulgences were obtainable by pilgrims to Compostela once a year (presumably on 25 July) in the second half of the 14C (citing Purchas's pilgrim of 1422 in support) (8), but that compostelan holy years and the jubilee indulgences specifically attached to them date only from 1428. Once again, Compostela was following the lead of Rome, where a holy year carrying a jubilee indulgence had been celebrated in 1423. Thereafter -- verified by the testimony of the many 15th century pilgrims whose accounts have survived – compostelan jubilees were celebrated in 1434, 1445, 1451, 1456 and so on, with a few hiccups due to plague, war and political considerations, down to our own day. It is apparent from what is related by William Wey in 1456 that the jubilee was by then being celebrated in much the same way as it is today, and that the institution of it was even then being attributed to a privilege granted by Calixtus II (9).

Storrs makes the point that in the 15th century few pilgrims from England sailed except in jubilee years (10). Pilgrimage over land went on in a steady stream, of course, but given the importance placed on gaining the promised indulgence, was very likely much greater in jubilee years than ordinarily, as it is today. It is a fair assumption that a heightened sense of devotion would have led many pilgrims to try to be present for the feast of the Apostle on 25 July, celebrated in the cathedral with great solemnity. (The winter date of the feast of the Translation of St James's relics – 30 December - may have kept numbers down, even in holy years).

I do not propose to say much about the ceremonial surrounding holy years or feast-days, about which it is difficult to find two authorities in agreement (11). Ordinarily pilgrims entered the cathedral by the north door, or *Puerta Francigena,* but once holy years became established, ceremonial came to surround the opening and closing of the *Puerta Santa* or *Puerta del Perdón.* According to some scholars, this door, opening off the lower part of the *Plaza de Quintana,* was Aymeric Picaud's *Puerta Sancto Pelagio,* the entrance to the cathedral used by the monks of the nearby monastery of San Pelayo de Antealtares. The evolution of its name may owe something to the change in the site of hearing pilgrims' confessions, from earlier centuries, in the chapel of the *Corticela,* to the chapel of *El Salvador,* which immediately adjoined the door in question, at the east end of the cathedral and directly behind the high altar (12). The Holy Door itself is more accurately two doors with a tiny passage between them: the inner, romanesque one, and the outer one opening onto the square, built in 1611 and remodelled in 1622. The well-loved statues of St James and his two companions, Theodore and Athanasius, date from 1694.

What I have not been able to find out is exactly when the ritual surrounding the opening and closing of the *Puerta Santa* at the beginning and end of the holy year took shape. A recent guidebook to Santiago is not alone in commenting that it takes place 'according to an antique ceremonial' - which does not shed much light on the matter.

Whether in ordinary years or holy years, in the middle ages the cathedral would have been thoroughly cleaned in the week preceding St James's feast-day, decorated with tapestries and the finest hangings, and the floor strewn with herbs. Pilgrims wishing to spend the eve of the feast in the customary vigil in the cathedral were expected to purchase a candle from one of the sellers of devotional articles whose stalls lined the *Plaza de la Azabacheria,* and enter the cathedral with them lit (the candles were supposed to last from nightfall until the end of the first mass in the morning). The vigil was spent standing (13). (The night vigil was not, in fact, restricted to holy years or to the eve of the feast-day, but was habitually enacted by pilgrims on the night of their arrival, and for this reason the *Liber Sancti Jacobi* reports that the doors of the cathedral stood open 'day and night'.) Especially in a holy year, the crowding would have been intense. It is doubtful whether, after about the middle of the 12th century, pilgrims had free access to the crypt where the relics of the Apostle were guarded. But there was competition to get as close to the crypt and the relics as possible, and we can infer that the resulting scrum was not for the feeble of bone or resolve.

It was not, of course, enough just to be there to gain the longed-for jubilee. Much importance was attached to the pilgrim's offering to St James and donation to the cathedral fabric, his promise to do a work of charity, and his prayers for the intentions of the Roman Pontiff. The most important aspect, however, was his sincere penitence, his purification through sacramental confession, and his conversion to new life through sharing in holy communion. Pilgrims had ample opportunity to prepare themselves for confession during their journeys and the night's vigil. They made their confessions before mass and holy communion. (Only later did they venerate the relics of St James, being conducted to the crypt by one of the cathedral canons.) For foreign pilgrims, confession was facilitated by clerics speaking various languages and known as *lenguajeros or linguaria.* The sacrament took place in the chapel of *El Salvador* mentioned earlier, which was rededicated to the king of France in 1380 following a generous endowment (14). The late Dr William Melczer and others have pointed out the significance of the location of this chapel: it is the easternmost, and the largest, located directly behind the high altar, and is flanked by chapels dedicated respectively to St John and St Peter, who with St James constituted the 'inner circle' of apostles, and witnessed the most significant moments of Christ's earthly life (15).

Here, in this holiest of sites after the crypt and the high altar, pilgrims were also issued with a certificate of having completed the pilgrimage (16). The earliest surviving example of one of these documents dates from the early 14th century (17). It seems to have originated as an official substitute for the commonly purchased souvenirs, such as badges and scallop-shells, which pilgrims bought in such quantities in the environs of the cathedral (18). Such *insignia,* as these souvenirs came to be called (since they were seen as 'proof', like the lead seals more properly called *insignia*, fixed to documents and mentioned below), had come to be falsified and fraudulently sold to pilgrims who, for a host of reasons, might wish to be seen to have completed their pilgrimages but who in fact had not. Pilgrims ranged from those serving civil or ecclesiastical punishments, to vagabonds passing themselves off as pilgrims to take advantage of strangers' openhandedness. There were endless canonical and civil penalties intended to protect the value of *insignia,* but counterfeits were nonetheless very common. Pope Innocent III, in a bull dated 18 June 1207 and sent to all the bishops of Spain and Gascony, excommunicated those who falsified *insignia.* In 1259, Alexander IV issued a bull ordering that shell-badges be made in Compostela under the control of the cathedral chapter.

Pilgrims' motives for wanting a dated proof of pilgrimage were varied. In the case of those impelled along the Way of St James by the force of law, the reason is patent. Similarly, those being paid to undertake a 'proxy' pilgrimage on behalf of someone else, needed proof that the contract had been fulfilled to collect the payment or favour due to them. Some confraternities demanded proof of having reached Compostela before accepting newly returned pilgrims as members. Exemption from certain taxes was a privilege conceded by some towns to returning pilgrims on proof of status (19).

The evolution of the actual certificate is in itself very interesting. In the 14th century it was similar to a letter of diplomatic accreditation: handwritten on parchment, and signed on behalf of the cathedral chapter by the senior cardinal or canon, known as the *Penitenciario.* Next to his signature was affixed the wax seal of the altar of Santiago, impressed over narrow cords held together by small lead *insignia.* The pilgrim's pious intention was attested to and his right to the *insignia* affirmed.

The proceedings of the meetings of the cathedral chapter dating from the late 15th century reveal the organisation that by that time went into providing services for pilgrims. Besides the confessors, the clerics in charge of showing relics and those who accepted the offerings, the senior cardinal was assisted by a veritable scriptorium of copiers, and a *latinero de los sellos,* or seal-affixer. A Polish pilgrim of 1581 left the following description of his 'letter' or 'passport': 'written on parchment with the *insignia* of the senior cardinal attached, for which two *reales* was paid; they also added a little proof of confession for which one *cuarto was* paid' (20). The advent of the printing press in time made the production of 'letters of proof' much faster and simpler, since it was necessary only to write the name of the pilgrim, the date and a few adaptations of the Latin text. At some time in the 17th century, the document came to include an integral certification of confession and holy communion, which had until then been slips of pasted-on paper or stamps.

The document, known earlier as a *compostelana* and later as a *compostela,* was by now usually printed on paper in gothic lettering, and measured about 18 by 24 cms. In the top left corner was a small woodcut showing St James as a pilgrim, complete with hat, staff and satchel (21). Only very grand certificates continued to be hand-written on parchment and could include, as text, more or less what the relevant personage and the canon writing it wanted to say. The text of the standard printed document altered only slightly over the centuries. One such alteration took place in response to a dispute that arose when, as a result of courtly pressure from Madrid, a papal declaration made St Teresa of Avila co-patroness of Spain with St James. The cathedral chapter in Santiago protested strongly and added the words 'sole and only' to the phrase on the *compostela* referring to the patronage of St James. The text was later expanded to include more about the pious motives of the pilgrims. In the mid-18th century the printed border of oak leaves was added and the picture of the Apostle changed to show a seated figure; the seal of the altar of St James was by now only a printed reproduction. In 1775 the mention of 'sole and only' patronage was removed and the phrase 'St James, Apostle to us and of Spain the Patron' added; the resulting text has lasted almost unchanged until the present day (22). The main elements of the modem document continue to be, firstly, the words setting out the power of the cathedral chapter and its representative to concede the certificate; secondly, the statement honouring the Apostle and stating the named pilgrim's devout intentions in visiting his shrine; and thirdly, the canonical signature, date and inked seal. Since early this century - but no-one seems to know exactly when - the border decorated with jacobean motifs has been more elaborate but still includes the original oak leaves, and St James has reverted to being *Santiago Peregrino*. In 1994 the seal showing him as *Matamoros* was abandoned in favour of the ancient one showing the star over his tomb, probably to accord better with the theme of reconciliation that has been so emphasized in recent years by both Rome and the Church in Spain.

Reverting to the 14th and 15th centuries, it is clear that the functions of the *compostela* gradually came to exceed the mere verification of *insignia.* The *Liber Sancti Jacobi* had affirmed that 'Indeed, all poor pilgrims must, on the first night that follows the day of their arrival at the altar of the Blessed James, receive at the hospice, for the love of God and the Apostle, full hospitality' (23). But with the great growth of the pilgrimage, the hospices were frequently overrun, and hospitality, in Santiago and elsewhere, often abused. The *compostela* came to have the additional function of separating false from genuine pilgrims. There were so many of the former flooding into the city by

D. Joannes Martinez Bretal
huius Almae Apostolicae et Metropolitanae Ecclesiae Compostellanae Dignitas Decani et sigilli Altaris Beati Jacobi Apostoli custos, ut omnibus Fidelibus et Peregrinis ex toto terrarum Orbe, devotionis affectu vel voti causa, ad limina Apostoli Nostri Hispaniarum Patroni ac Tutelaris **SANCTI JACOBI** convenientibus, authenticas visitationis litteras expediat, omnibus et singulis praesentes inspecturis, notum facio:
Laurie Dennett
hoc sacratissimum Templum pietatis causa devote visitasse. In quorum fidem praesentes litteras, nomine meo subscriptas et sigilo ejusdem Sanctae Ecclesiae munitas, ei confero.
Datum Compostellae die 10 mensis junii
anno Dñi 1976

Jose M Díaz

The author's 'compostela', signed by the dean of Santiago cathedral, since in 1986 there was as yet no Pilgrim Office.

the late 15th century that they were forbidden to remain there longer than a few days unless they were ill. The genuine pilgrim could present his *compostela* to a notary, and thus engrossed, the document gave permission to remain longer. (Santiago's *Hospital Real*, still a recent foundation in the mid-16th century, was by then marking the staves of pilgrims so that they did not overstay their allotted time (24). At the end of the 17th century, the Hospital of St James in Bordeaux tightened up the rules to prevent vagabonds from availing themselves of the attentions reserved for pilgrims to Compostela. Those on their way had to show the letter from their parish priest, and those returning, proof of having made their confession in the cathedral. The porter was required to write down the name, dates of arrival and departure, and place of origin of each pilgrim (25). In these measures we see the beginnings of the modem-day *credencial.*

The *compostela* had uses outside the city of the Apostle, besides merely proving that the bearer had been there. Since pilgrims in earlier centuries had to return home by the same means as they arrived, the *compostela* may have served as an additional form of safe-conduct, especially if the return journey took their owners off the established routes where they enjoyed considerable legal protection. Whether on the well-worn pilgrim roads or farther afield, the possession of a *compostela* may have resulted in spontaneous offers of meals, beds and favours from local people that eased the homeward way. The rules of the religious foundations at Roncesvalles and Aubrac allowed for the special treatment of accredited pilgrims on their way home, which included warm water for washing and better wine (26). At the hospitals attached to other shrines that might be visited on the return journey - Oviedo, San Millán de la Cogolla, Santo Domingo de Silos or Montserrat - those who had been to Compostela were bound to have been favoured visitors.

For the uses to which it could be put, then, the *compostela* became a desirable piece of paper. For one thing, as Pablo Arribas Briones points out so eloquently in his *Picaros y Picaresca en el Camino de Santiago* (and I translate),

> *'...the fact of having made one of the major pilgrimages, such as the one to Compostela, gave one a boost up the social ladder. The person who had been to Finisterre was an initiate into mysteries, knowledgeable about far-off lands (about which he could speak, capturing the attention of an ever-credulous audience) to the point of acquiring charisma. People respected him and considered him 'a somebody'. Perhaps no-one has yet studied with enough attention what was implied in this change of attitude and even status in a society as closed as was the historic age of the pilgrimages, and what that could mean in the lives of some who had worn the pilgrim habit.' (27)*

Not surprisingly, since the subject of Don Pablo's book is the low-life of the Way of St James, the forged and ill-gotten *compostela* receives a mention. To cater to that desire for enhanced standing just referred-to, that longing for access to privilege and hospitality, the criminal element carried on a thriving trade throughout the middle ages in stolen documents, for which there was no shortage of ready buyers. In some countries, possession of a *compostela* carried privileges; apparently, among the Slovaks, those who could prove that they had been to Compostela in three consecutive years were free from taxes for the rest of their lives (28), which goes some way to explaining the degree of ceremony and organisation that groups of pilgrims from that area are recorded as having observed. In Compostela itself, the cathedral had rivals that specialised in the production of fake certificates and insignia (some *alcaldes* of the city are known to have sold *compostelas*); their market was the army of false pilgrims mentioned above. At least the forgeries produced locally must have borne enough resemblance to the real thing to be convincing. To so-called 'pilgrims' who had no intention of going any farther along the Way of St James than the verdant hills of La Rioja, anything could be sold, since they were unlikely ever to have seen a real *compostela.*

What the *compostela* could actually be worth in the hands of a rascal, even if he were a *bone fide* pilgrim, can be illustrated by the case of the 18th century Frenchman Guillaume Manier, who had provisioned himself with at least three safe-conducts before setting out on his pilgrimage (29), and on arrival obtained his *compostela* for the price of two *sueldos.* He and his companions lost no time in seeking to recoup their outlay, but went straight away to the archbishop's palace to beg alms, each being given a *cuarto.* Manier subsequently spent some time as a mendicant pilgrim in the company of a blind fiddler, managing to collect no less than fifty *sueldos* through the adroit use of his *compostela* (30).

It is interesting to note the changes brought about in the appreciation of the document since the introduction of the pilgrim *credencial* by the first *Amigos del Camino de Santiago* in Estella in 1962. Although this familiar item was devised by the late Dr Francisco Berguete, it was initially authorised and signed by the Archbishop of Santiago de Compostela, and as the pilgrimage began to grow,

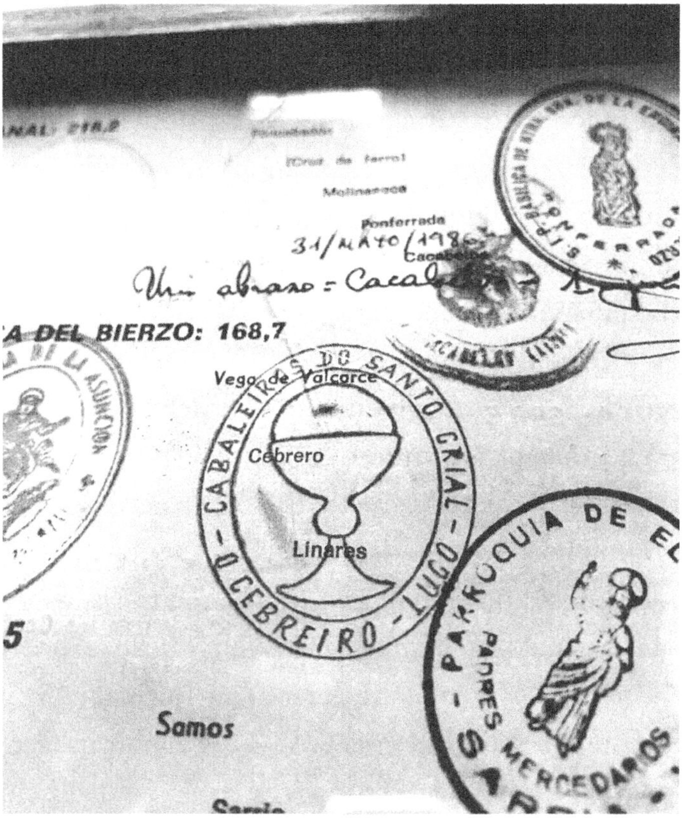

The 'sello' or stamp from O Cebreiro in the author's 'credencial' or pilgrim passport, given to her in Estella by Francisco Berguete - the founder, back in 1962, of Spain's first association of 'Amigos del Camino'.

responsibility for producing it passed to the cathedral chapter. Today it is the *credencial*, or pilgrim passport, duly filled out and stamped at the various stopping places along the *Camino*, which gives access to hospitality *en route* to Santiago as once the *compostela* did on the way home. That the *credencial* does this on the journey *to* the shrine makes it a distant successor of the safe-conduct, and that is one reason why it provides a space for the pilgrim's parish priest or bishop to write something concerning the motive for undertaking the pilgrimage. On arrival in Santiago, the stamped and dated *credencial* and a brief personal testimony before the *hospitaleros* at the Pilgrim Office will result in the issuing of the personalised and dated *compostela.*

There is a degree of misunderstanding about both the standard *credencial* and the *compostela* which needs dispelling. Both documents are issued - and that means produced and paid for - by the cathedral chapter. In the case of the *credencial* there is also a hefty postage bill (only sometimes reimbursed) as it is distributed all over Spain, to *refugios*, to churches both on and off the pilgrim routes and to the associations of *Amigos* for them to pass on. Many pilgrims today believe that they have a "right" to the *compostela* through the fact of having made the pilgrimage and faithfully stamped their *credenciales.* This is not, in fact, the case. What any pilgrim *does* have a right to is the *credencial* itself, since it does not depend on being a member of anything - and in this sense it is more freely available than the Confraternity's own pilgrim passport. If your motives for walking or cycling the Camino are not religious or, as many people prefer to call them nowadays, 'spiritual', the *credencial* can simply act as a means of identifying yourself as a pilgrim, and having obtained one wherever in Spain you begin your journey, you can fill in the details yourself, as fully or as minimally as you please, and get it stamped where you like at your stops. There is a handsome coloured certificate with a Latin text awarded by the cathedral and available at the Pilgrim Office that will attest to your having reached your destination.

But if you want the *compostela,* which is still, as it always has been, the witness to having made the pilgrimage for devotional reasons, it *will* matter where you get your *credencial* stamped and what you say on presenting it at the Pilgrim Office. The pilgrimage, undertaken as such, is a journey *to the tomb of St James.* You will not obtain the *compostela*, however far you have come, unless you fulfil this condition, and so you must walk *the last hundred kilometres* into Santiago, or cycle *the last two hundred*, and stamp your *credencial* so as to make it clear that you have done this. (Recently, in response to much abuse of the system, the Pilgrim Office has been demanding *two* stamps per day over the required minimum distances.) The traditional sources of stamps in any given town are the parish church, the *ayuntamiento* or town hall, and the *cuartel* of the *guardia civil.* Most hotels, restaurants and bars have devised their own stamps in recent years, almost as part of the welcome offered to pilgrims. It is fine to include some of these, but inadvisable to fill up your whole *credencial* with what looks to the Pilgrim Office like the evidence of an 800-kilometre wine-tasting.

Similarly, it is helpful to find a simple form of words in advance that will confirm that your pilgrimage has indeed been a spiritual quest. It is unusual to be asked what denomination you are, or even - surprisingly - whether you are Christian. It is very, very rare for anyone who has completed the required distance to be refused the *compostela,* and when such instances arise, it is nearly always because someone has spread out a *credencial* full of bar stamps and given “time in the open air” or “gastronomy” as his motive for journeying to Compostela. If that is in fact the case, he should be asking for, and will certainly be given, the certificate, and should be satisfied with it.

Notes

1. Any good encyclopaedia will draw upon these Old Testament references to trace the history of the 'jubilee' and the 'sabbath'. Addis and Arnold's *Catholic Dictionary*, revised by Mgr. P E Hallett, London 1951, is concise and clear on each topic.
2. See the *Catechism of the Catholic Church* (London 1994), 1471-1480, pp 331-333.
3. See Richard Fletcher, *St James's Catapult: the Life and Times of Diego Gelmírez of Santiago de Compostela*. Santiago de Compostela, 1984.
4. See Fernando López Alsina, 'Años Santos Romanos y Años Santos Compostelanos' in *Santiago, Roma, Jerusalén*. Actas del III Congreso Internacional de Estudios Jacobeos (1997). Santiago de Compostela, 1999; pp 213-242.
5. Besides the article cited above, see López Alsina's 'El Papa Alejandro III confirma el Jubileo de la Iglesia de Santiago' in *Santiago, Camino de Europa: Culto y Cultura en la Peregrinación a Compostela* ed. Serafín Moralejo and Fernando López Alsina, Madrid 1993. See also Antonio López Ferreiro, *Historia de la S. A. M. Iglesia de Santiago de Compostela* IV, p 329.
6. López Alsina, 'Años Santos...' p 216; López Ferreiro, Append. 28, pp 73-74.
7. Constance Mary Storrs, *Jacobean Pilgrims from England to St James of Compostela from the early twelfth to the late fifteenth century*. Santiago de Compostela, 1994. pp 113-114.

8. López Alsina, 'Años Santos…' pp 230-237. Robert Brian Tate and Thorlac Turville-Petrie, *Two Pilgrim Itineraries of the Later Middle Ages*. Santiago de Compostela, 1994. pp 38-39, 53.
9. Since this paper was delivered, the Confraternity of Saint James has published Francis Davey's *William Wey, an English Pilgrim to Compostela in 1456*. London, 2000. But see also López Alsina, 'Años Santos…', pp 235-236.
10. Storrs, p 111.
11. The best summary of the procedure in Santiago can be found under 'Año Santo' in the *Gran Enciclopedia Gallega*. 30 vols. Santiago, 1974.
12. James Hogarth, tr., *The Pilgrim's Guide: a 12th Century Guide for the Pilgrim to Santiago de Compostela*. Confraternity of Saint James, London 1992. p 63.
13. Luis Vázquez de Parga, José María Lacarra and Juan Uria Ríu, *Las Peregrinaciones a Santiago de Compostela*. (Facsimile edition of that published in 1948 by the Consejo Superior de Investigaciones Científicas, Madrid) 3 vols. Instituto Principe de Viana, Pamplona, 1993. Vol. 1, p 146.
14. *ibid.* pp 147-154.
15. William Melczer, *The Pilgrim's Guide to Santiago de Compostela*. New York, 1993; pp 196-197, note 393; pp 213-214, note 501.
16. For one of the many pilgrim accounts of receiving the *compostela*, see that of Domenico Laffi: James Hall, *A Journey to the West: the diary of a seventeenth-century pilgrim from Bologna to Santiago de Compostela*. Leiden and Santiago de Compostela, 1997, p 164.
17. Cited in Vázquez de Parga, vol. 1, p 152, note 89. The document in question was dated 1 May 1321 and attested to the second pilgrimage of one Yves le Breton.

18. See the two-part article by Francisco-Cristóbal Fernández Sánchez, 'La Compostela. Una Certificación Multisecular' in *Compostela* no. 3 (May 1994) pp 12-15, and no. 4 (October 1994) pp 17-20.
19. See part 1 of the article previously cited, in *Compostela* no 3 (May 1994) p 14.
20. Cited by Fernández Sánchez, above, part 1 p 15, and by Vázquez de Parga, vol 1 p 153, from J. Liske, 'Viajes de Extranjeros por España y Portugal en los siglos XV, XVI and XVII', translated into Spanish by F. Rozanski, Madrid (n.d.).
21. Fernández Sánchez, part 1, p 15.
22. Fernández Sánchez, part 2, p 18.
23. Melczer, p 62.
24. Vázquez de Parga, vol. 1, p 313.
25. Pablo Arribas Briones, *Picaros y Picaresca en el Camino de Santiago*. Burgos, 1993. p 256.
26. *ibid.*, p 255. It is interesting to note that while returning pilgrims were allowed three days' stay and generous meals at Roncesvalles, the indigent poor and 'vagabonds' were only permitted one, with, seemingly, a more modest dinner and breakfast. See Vázquez de Parga, vol. I, p 338 n.
27. Arribas Briones, p 253.
28. *loc. cit.*
29. Elias Valiña Sampedro, *El Camino de Santiago. Estudio Histórico-Juridico*. 2nd. ed., Diputación de Lugo, 1990. pp 26-27.
30. Arribas Briones, p 255.

10

Pilgrimage to Santiago de Compostela from the British Isles. Originally written as an entry entitled 'Reino Unido' for the *Gran Enciclopedia del Camino de Santiago. Diccionario de la Cultura Jacobea.* (ed. Manuel Fernández Rodríguez), vol. 15. Ediciones Bolanda, Santiago de Compostela, 2010.

For the inhabitants of the British Isles of more than a thousand years ago, the sea not only separated their country from the continent, but also facilitated their contacts with it. Since the age of the seafaring Phoenicians and the Romans, the Bay of Biscay had linked these islands to the Iberian peninsula as much as it had acted as a barrier. British mariners knew to avoid the so-called 'Coast of Death', or 'Costa da Morte' of Galicia, but in general, the northwestern region of Spain was known not only as *finis terrae*, as it was to the navigators of other countries, but also for ports like Coruña and Vigo that were halts on the voyage to the Mediterranean.

Given the well-known Anglo-Saxon predilection for pilgrimage, it would be surprising if, in addition to Rome and other holy sites, these Germanic settlers did not also go on pilgrimage to Santiago in the era before the Norman Conquest in 1066. None the less, as the historian Derek Lomax tells us in his article *The First English Pilgrims to Santiago de Compostela* (1985), it seems that the first visitor to Santiago who can be identified with England was the Anglo-Norman nobleman Walter Gifford, in 1064, shortly before the Conquest. More properly 'English' was St. Godric of Finchale (d. 1170), who was both mariner and merchant before becoming a pilgrim. According to a biographical account, he visited many holy places, including Jerusalem and Santiago, in 1102, before retiring to a valley near Durham in 1110 to live out his days as a hermit.

The figure of Godric illustrates the essential characteristic of pilgrimage to Santiago from the British Isles: not just the need to cross the Channel, but also the option of travelling by sea. One could sail all the way to Galicia, or disembark at one of the continental Atlantic ports and walk or ride the rest of the way. A pilgrim could also choose to go by sea in one direction, and overland in the other, as in the case of the Bishop of Winchester, Henry of Blois, who arrived in Santiago after a sea journey from Rome in 1151. But Dr. Lomax also indicates other examples, mainly from the first half of the 12th century, of Anglo-Norman nobles who made their pilgrimages to Santiago by passing through France and across Spain.

Sometimes, in thanks for the hospitality they received in monasteries along the way, these pilgrims gave properties in England to these religious houses. Such gifts are occasionally mentioned in documents preserved in French monasteries, as at Sainte-Marie de la Sauve Majeure, near Bordeaux. Among the noble pilgrims were Richard Mauleverer of Yorkshire, Ansgot de la Haye from Lincolnshire, Hugh Montgomery, earl of Shrewsbury, Oliver de Merlimond, Mortimer's chief steward and lord of Wigmore, and Waleran de Beaumont, count of Meulan in Normandy and earl of Worcester in England.

The case of Oliver de Merlimond is especially interesting: he gave to the canons of St. Victor in Paris the church that he was constructing at Shobden, in Herefordshire. This church (today in ruins), and others in the same area share sculptural characteristics that show the influence of sculptures from the cathedral of Santiago and other churches on the routes from England to Compostela. For this reason it seems probable that Merlimond was accompanied by a sculptor or artist, who later employed in the Herefordshire churches the elements that he had seen and drawn on his travels.

Many of the noble pilgrims of the 12th century are known today through research in the cartularies, or documents listing church property, of which English archives have large collections. There were many British pilgrims from every social class of whom nothing is known, because there is no documentary evidence of them. It is possible the London properties acquired by the monastery-hospital of Santa Maria of Roncesvalles (such as the hospital of Charing Cross, and St. Mary's church, Aylward) were donated by pilgrims, though it is not known who these were, or the dates of the gifts. To obtain a more vivid sense of who went on pilgrimage from the British Isles, we must take a look at the collections of the miracles of English saints such as St. Godric, St. Gilbert of Sempringham, St. Thomas Becket,

St. William of Norwich, and St. Frideswide. These contain accounts of people who made vows to St. James: those cured of illnesses or saved from storms and other dangers though his intervention, and those who took to the road to fulfill penances or legally imposed sentences.

This abundance of documentary evidence, and the broad range of monuments and medieval dedications that survive, makes it clear that devotion to St. James was widely established throughout the British Isles well before the 13th century. The focus of much of this devotion was a relic of the holy Apostle: a hand, brought to England in 1125 by Matilda, daughter of king Henry I, and widow of the Holy Roman Emperor Henry V. The great abbey of Reading, of which today only ruins remain, was built by Henry I to house this relic. Many miracles were attributed to it, and thousands of pilgrims venerated it every year until the abbey was destroyed in the 16th century. A mummified hand in a small casket, found in the ruins some 130 years ago, is today kept in the sacristy of St. Peter's church, Marlow-on-Thames, near Reading, and can be seen on written request.

As Dr. Brian Tate has written in *Pilgrimages to Saint James of Compostella from the British Isles during the Middle Ages* (1990; republished by the Confraternity of Saint James, 2005), to understand the changing circumstances of these pilgrimages, it is necessary to consider them in the political and economic contexts of their age. The relative decline in Muslim maritime power, and the complicated relations among England, France and Castille from the 13th to the 15th centuries, each had important consequences for pilgrims from the British Isles. The most meaningful change seems to have been the notable increase in the number of pilgrims travelling by sea. Evidence of this is found in the series – unique among European archive sources – of royal licences awarded to the owners and captains of English ships, authorising them to transport pilgrims to Santiago.

Although this traffic owed something to existing commercial links (wine, textiles) between England and the continental ports, the main business was transporting pilgrims to Galicia and back again. Bristol, the Cornish ports of St. Ives, Penzance, and Fowey, and those of the English south coast (Plymouth, Dartmouth, Bournemouth, Poole, Southampton), together with Galway, Waterford, Wexford and Dublin in Ireland and Pembroke in Wales, were the major points of embarcation. Very likely, Scottish pilgrims embarked at the ports of Clyde, Forth or Tay, or trekked to Newcastle.

The detailed study of licences carried out by Constance M. Storrs (*Jacobean Pilgrims from England to St. James of Compostella from the Early Twelfth to the Late Fifteenth Centuries*, 1994; republished by the Confraternity of Saint James, 1998) shows that (although the first licence is dated 1235) pilgrim traffic by sea really began to increase from 1350, and continued to do so until the middle of the 15th century. The high point came in 1434, a Compostellan Holy Year, in which 70 licences were granted, but other Holy Years (1428, 1445, 1451, 1456) were also high points. In general, the ships that carried pilgrims were small, and in many cases, belonged to their captains. They could carry between 30 and 400 pilgrims per voyage. Assuming an average figure of 60 pilgrims per ship, the total number of pilgrims carried by sea in the second half of the 14th century works out to about 5000, whereas the corresponding figure for the first half of the 15th century would be 14,000 – almost three times as many.

The routes taken by pilgrims to reach the ports were, for the most part, such ordinary public thoroughfares as then existed, usually the successors of the Roman roads. Two stand out as preferred routes: One was the road from Reading, where the famous relic of St. James could be venerated, to the port at Southampton. The other was the well-known 'Salt route' between Droitwich and Bristol, the city most closely associated with English maritime and mercantile power, from which many ships departed for Spain's northern ports. Frequently, to protect themselves from the pirates that operated freely in the continent's coastal waters, the ships sailed in convoy. When they could, Irish ships joined the convoys sailing from English ports, so as to cross the Bay of Biscay in greater safety. With good weather and a favourable wind, it was possible to make the journey from England to Coruña in six days. On the other hand, an unlucky pilgrim ship could remain becalmed for weeks, awaiting the weather conditions that would allow it to leave port.

The sea voyage was shorter, and free of some of the risks pilgrims faced if travelling overland, such as robbery, rapacious toll-collectors, or sudden political conflict, but it was by no means easy, or particularly pleasant. Accommodations on board were cramped and ill-ventilated. Seasickness, storms, and pirates could strike at any moment. Despite all that, in contrast with the six months needed to walk to Santiago and back via France, the maritime option clearly had its attractions.

No resume of the history of British pilgrimage would be complete without mention of the many literary works it inspired. The 15th century sea voyages generated compositions as diverse as the anonymous poem *The Pilgrims Sea Voyage and Sea Sickness* (which portrayed the discomforts of life aboard ship in graphic terms), the autobiographical account of the mystic, Margery Kempe (who sailed to Compostela in 1417 to fulfil a vow), and the *Itineraries* of William Wey (a master of Eton College, in which the author described his pilgrimages to Santiago, Rome and Jerusalem). Later, in the collection of narratives published in 1625 by Samuel Purchas as *Purchas His Pilgrims*, there appeared another anonymous poem, about a journey in 1425, by sea to Bordeaux and from there overland to Compostela. The personal accounts written by Robert Langton and Andrew Boorde also supply the literature of pilgrimage with much information about the experience in the late 15th and early 16th centuries.

The Protestant Reformation and the creation of the Anglican church were harsh blows to the British impulse to go on pilgrimage, and it never really recovered. The worsening of relations between England and Spain during the reigns of Elizabeth I and Phillip II had the effect of damaging for centuries the traditional friendship between the two countries. It was only recovered when they found themselves allied against Napoleon, and even after that, it was a long time before the British again became interested in the pilgrimage to Santiago. When they did, their newfound curiosity owed more to the desire to travel fostered by 'agents' such as Thomas Cook than to any religious motivation. This attitude was strengthened by earlier 19th century writers such as Robert Southey and Richard Ford, who viewed the pilgrimage with scepticism, and George Borrow, who in *The Bible in Spain* described Santiago as beautiful but derelict, and the pilgrimage as an outdated and superstitious custom.

In the 20th century, the rebirth of interest in the pilgrimage, its routes and traditions, has been one component among many in the general fascination with everything medieval, and, since the Civil War, with Spain itself. The example of the French association, the *Amis du Chemin de Saint-Jacques*, founded in Paris in 1950, and of a similar organisation, the *Amigos del Camino de Santiago*, established in Estella, Navarre, in 1962, prompted the setting up of many more associations inside and outside Spain during the 1980s. Among these was the Confraternity of Saint James, which came into being when the six British members of the French *Amis* met in London on 13 January, 1983.

The Confraternity's stated aims were to inform and educate the British public about the pilgrimage, to provide prospective pilgrims with advice and practical help, and to identify, recover and study the jacobean heritage in the British Isles. To further these objectives, it has created a well-stocked Library, open to the public. It organises an annual programme of talks and other events, produces a range of publications and translations, (including guides to all the routes in France and Spain), and runs regular 'Practical Pilgrim' days around the country. Its growing series of 'county guides' is identifying the British place-names, monuments and works of art relating to the pilgrimage.

The Confraternity has also financed the reconstruction of two pilgrim albergues in Spain: one in the village of Rabanal del Camino in the mountains of Leon, the other in Miraz, in the province of Lugo, Galicia. Both are staffed by teams of trained volunteer wardens, or *hospitaleros*, drawn from the ranks of the Confraternity and of many other jacobean associations. Twenty-five years after its foundation, 'the CSJ' has more than 2,000 members in the United Kingdom and around the world. Although the majority of those who make their pilgrimages from the British Isles today travel overland, the Confraternity keeps alive the memory of those medieval sea journeys, and in 1999 even recreated one, hiring two historic ships to sail from Cornwall to Galicia, with 40 members aboard. They then walked to Santiago along the 'Camino Ingles', as their medieval predecessors would have, and received their *compostelas*.

As of 2010, the United Kingdom stood ninth in a country by country ranking of the annual number of pilgrims receiving the compostela.

11

2000 Years of the Camino de Santiago: Where Did It Come From? Where Is It Going? *A paper presented at the Gathering of Pilgrims in Toronto, Canada, on 14 May 2005, jointly organised by the Canadian Company of Pilgrims and American Pilgrims on the Camino.*

Thank you for inviting me to address this Gathering of Pilgrims from all over North America. It is a great pleasure to be here, and to be back in my native city.

"2000 Years of the Camino de Santiago: Where Did It Come From? Where Is It Going?" If I am to give an overview of such a long period in 45 minutes, I will have to get my walking boots on, so to speak. The title, perhaps, needs a word of explanation. I could have begun at what might seem the logical starting point, the discovery of the tomb of St James in the early 9th century, and carried on from there. But that would have left out the development of the literary tradition through which, as scholars such as Professor Manuel Díaz y Díaz and

Dr Robert Plötz have termed it, the "discovery-invention" of the tomb of St James came to be seen by contemporaries not only as plausible, but also as the culmination of long-held expectations. Moreover, had I begun in the ninth century, the political factors underlying the growth of the pilgrimage to the shrine of St James might not have been fully appreciated.

These considerations led me to conclude that the 'Way of Saint James', for our purposes, should include not just how pilgrims through the centuries, including ourselves, came to go there, but how and why people came to expect to find the relics of the Apostle where they did. How did this amazing journey – which unites us, not just to one another but to those pilgrims of centuries past – come to exist, evolve, enjoy a tremendous, pan-European glory, fade and nearly die, and revive to become what it is today? If I have been too ambitious in trying to answer that, I may run over my allotted time, but I doubt that I will bore you!

I think it is worth recapitulating what we know about the apostle James, usually called 'the Great', to distinguish him from other important figures in the early Church who were also called James. The Gospels tell us that James and his brother John the Evangelist were fishermen, like their father Zebedee, and that they left their nets, boat, father and all, when Christ told them to follow him. Later, with Peter, they formed a kind of inner circle of the apostles, sharing some of the most significant moments of Christ's earthly life: certain miracles, the Transfiguration, and the long night watch in the Garden of Gethsemane. If, like their fellow-apostle, Peter, they sometimes revealed a purely human understanding of events, their faith, like his, eventually transformed these limitations into strengths. Perhaps in their impulsiveness they took after their mother, who asked that her sons be seated at the right and left of the Master. His reply to her prefigured events to come, at least for James. The Acts of the Apostles relate how James was indeed the first to drink the cup of martyrdom, since he was beheaded on the orders of king Herod Agrippa in the year 44 A.D.. We have corroboration, and a touching description of this last event, from Clement of Alexandria, writing in about 200 A.D., who was repeating what his teacher Panteanus had been told by contemporaries of the apostles a generation earlier. Clement's account is quoted in the great *History of the Church* written by Eusebius of Caesarea early in the fourth century, and is, I think, worth reading to you, as it shows the formerly impetuous 'Son of Thunder' in a different light:

> *It appears that the guard who brought him into court was so moved when he saw him testify that he confessed that he, too, was a Christian. So they were both taken away together, and on the way he asked James to forgive him. James thought for a moment, then he said "I wish you peace", and kissed him. So both were beheaded at the same time.*

James's early death was presumably the reason he was not mentioned by Eusebius as having preached in a specific area of the world, as some of the other apostles were. Another early text suggested an area for James: the apocryphal 1st century *Gospel of the Twelve Holy Apostles*. This describes how, with the descent of the Holy Spirit at Pentecost, each apostle received the gift of the language corresponding to the land he was destined to evangelise. James was said to have been given Latin, which seemed to imply a destination in the west.

By the time of St Jerome, in the late 4th century, an exegetical tradition had developed which assumed that each apostle had died and was buried in the land where he had preached. There is logic in this: after all, in the face of the divine commandment to *Go out into all the world and proclaim the Good News*, it was hardly likely that an apostle would decide at some point that 'enough was enough' and return home! But James was known to have been martyred in Jerusalem, and so it would seem that he must have done exactly that. (As the late Dr William Melczer put it, *James's return to the Holy Land was tacitly understood in order to square his proselytising activities in Hispania with the evangelical account of his martyrdom in Judea*.)

Centuries later, the Apostle's death as related by Eusebius was included in the *Codex Calixtinus*, about which more will be said. It is usually known as the *passio modica* or 'lesser passion' of James, to distinguish it from a later, more elaborate account, compiled somewhere in the Rhone valley in the second half of the 5th century, which also was incorporated into the *Codex*. In that version the basic story was added to, with incidents such as James's struggle with the magician Hermogenes paralleling a similar event in the life of Peter, and a miraculous healing *en route* to his execution attesting to his divinely endowed gifts. This more elaborate account became known as the *passio magna*, or 'great passion' of James.

By the late sixth century, the *passio magna* was circulating as part of a collection of saints' lives and martyrdoms known as the *Breviarum Apostolorum*, or *Breviary of the Apostles*. This work was the first to claim that James had preached in the Roman province of Hispania, at the western extremity of the Mediterranean world. It also employed the phrase *archaia marmarica* ('marble sarcophagus') used in earlier Greek texts to refer to James's burial place. According to Professor Díaz y Díaz, the *Breviary* slightly altered it to emphasise the other meaning of *marmarica*, which was 'sea.' Therefore, James could be understood to have been buried 'in a place by the sea' somewhere in the west of Hispania.

The *Breviarum* became widely known in ecclesiastical circles during the seventh and eighth centuries, and the belief that James had preached and was buried in the west of Spain spread throughout Europe. Isidore of Seville's biographical study of Biblical figures, *De Ortu et Obitu Patrum*, written in about 630, mentions that James had evangelised the west of Spain. In Britain, the chronicler Aldhelm of Malmesbury, later bishop of Sherborne, wrote a poem in honour of James in 709 which claimed that he had *...converted the hispanic peoples with his teaching, converting the barbarous multitudes with divine words....*

A *Commentary on the Apocalypse* by the great defender of the Visigothic church, Beatus of Liébana, written in about 785, contained a list of the provinces of the world, each with its corresponding apostle, in which Hispania was allocated to James the Great. The famous hymn by the same author, *O Dei Verbum Patris*, alludes to 'the great Sons of Thunder' whose designated areas of preaching (since St John was known to have died in Asia Minor) spanned the Mediterranean: *John on the right who reigned over Asia and his brother, Spain.* The poem then recapitulates the *passio magna* and addresses St James in words that are still used today, every time the *botafumeiro* is swung in the cathedral in Santiago: *Oh most worthy and most holy apostle, shining golden chieftain of Spain, be our protector and patron on earth, warding off all ill, be our celestial health....*

And so, by the late eighth century, a literary tradition had developed which held that the burial place of the apostle James the Great lay in Spain, even if the site had not yet been identified. Interestingly, it was not until after the purported discovery of the tomb in about 814 that a corresponding tradition evolved concerning the Apostle's return to Palestine and death, and the transportation of his mortal remains back to Spain for burial. But very shortly - no more than 30 years after the acclaimed discovery - martyrologies by authors such as Florus of Lyons and Usuard of St Germaine-des-Prés were asserting that James's body had been returned to Spain and buried *contra mare Britannicum* or 'close to the British sea.' Such references lent credibility to the find, which from the moment of its occurrence received no less than royal confirmation. How and why did that come about?

Let us recall the prevailing political situation in the Iberian peninsula. Unlike the rest of it, the northwest had managed to resist the Moorish invasion from North Africa in the year 711 A.D. A century later, this area - the Christian kingdom of Asturias, which included a large part of modern-day Galicia - remained independent, sheltering behind the protective barrier of the mountains of León. It may have been besieged from the south, but the region was far from isolated, either politically or culturally, from the rest of Europe. The Roman road along the Cantabrian coast to the Pyrenees remained a major thoroughfare, while communications by sea allowed the Asturian kings, from their capital at Oviedo, to maintain close relations with Frankish rulers, and especially with the Carolingian court at Aachen.

Oveido, which housed the relics of San Salvador brought there by Visigothic churchmen fleeing the Muslim invasion, was already a place of pilgrimage. It also possessed the shrine of the *Siete Varones Apostolicos* or 'Seven Apostolic Youths', who were believed to have accompanied the apostle James during his time in Spain. From Oviedo, too, the vestiges of the Visigothic church, whose spokesman was the Beatus of Liébana mentioned above, denounced the compromises made with the invaders by the church hierarchy in occupied Toledo. If the church in Oviedo had a heightened awareness of its own role as custodian of doctrinal purity, the court of king Alfonso II was imbued with a corresponding sense of territorial mission. This could be realistically entertained because of powerful backing from beyond the Pyrenees and the Bay of Biscay.

It was in such a climate that the news of the "discovery-invention" of the tomb of the apostle James was announced. The story is well-known: how, in a secluded wood in the diocese of Iria Flavia near the Galician coast, a tomb was found, in misty circumstances that later gave rise to the legend of the monk Pelayo and his being guided to the spot by a star (the parallel with Christ's Nativity being fairly obvious). The find, a marble sarcophagus containing human remains, was at once acclaimed by the local bishop, Teodomir, as that of the apostle James the Great. Informed by the bishop of the discovery, king Alfonso II and his court set out in haste from Oviedo, probably taking the Roman road via Fonsagrada and Lugo – today's Camino Primitivo.

The king had a simple wooden church built at the site, thereby legitimising the story. His belief in it seems to have been genuine, in that he soon endowed the little church with all the land in a three mile radius around it, and on his deathbed left 500 coins of the purest gold to the shrine. His son Alfonso III replaced the small church with a larger and finer one, and granted permission for the founding nearby of the monasteries of San Pelayo de Antealtares and San Martín Pinario.

The ramifications of the discovery, and its royal recognition, are hard to overestimate. Alfonso II's journey - some claim him as the first "pilgrim to Santiago" - was the catalyst for local pilgrimage, which, like a ripple extending outward from a stone tossed into a pond, soon carried the news beyond the Asturian kingdom, drawing pilgrims from the Basque provinces and Navarra. The possession of apostolic relics - the only such treasure anywhere west of Rome, and moreover, the relics of the very apostle so long associated with Hispania - fortified the Asturian kingdom's strong Christian identity. It also strengthened (or, if one interprets the story up to now as more 'invention' than 'discovery', provided the justification for) its determination to regain territory lost more than a century earlier to the Moorish invaders.

The earliest phase of the *reconquista*, the movement to eject the Islamic conquerors from the *meseta* and the lands to the south, periodically overcame the interminable dynastic squabbles of the era to unite Christian forces across the north of the Peninsula. James was invoked as patron and protector. Victories were attributed to his aid, as at the Battle of Clavijo in 844, when the apostle was said to have appeared on a white horse to lead the charge against the Moors.

Pilgrimage to the apostle James's tomb was initially local, but the singular importance of the shrine was quickly communicated to the court of Louis the Pious at Aachen, and dukes and counts of the Frankish territories. From them it percolated into the noble houses, the cathedral schools and the monasteries. The first foreign pilgrim of whom there is any record was Gotescalc, Bishop of Le Puy, in 947, reflecting the close connection that Christian Spain already enjoyed with the Aquitaine and Auvergne regions of France. During this early period, pilgrims - whether from the free territories of Spain or from across the Pyrenees - made their way to Galicia via the Roman road along the Cantabrian coast, or from port to port in small boats along the coast itself, since the Roman road over the *meseta* (today's Camino Francés) was in Moorish hands. While some visited Oviedo and then continued westward by same route that Alfonso II had used, others stayed on the coast until they could turn inland over gentler terrain, on what we know nowadays as the main stem of the Camino del Norte.

Once the Ebro valley and the *meseta* were recaptured, royal privileges encouraged Franks to settle there and repopulate this 'no-man's land.' Dynastic links with the ruling houses across the Pyrenees meant that there was a steady interchange of ideas, doctrinal trends and appointments over the whole region. The relationship with the reformed Benedictine order of Cluny, begun by king Sancho *el Mayor* of Navarre late in the tenth century, continued under his descendants. His great-grandson Alfonso VI of Leon, who emerged victorious from wars against his brothers, added Galicia, Castile, and later La Rioja and Navarre to his own Leonese inheritance to create a solid bloc of territory across the north.

Alfonso VI's reign marked an important phase in the development of the pilgrimage to the tomb of James the Great. He invited the Benedictines of Cluny to establish a chain of monasteries and abbeys along the Roman thoroughfares that crossed the reconquered territories. We will recognise some of their names: Leyre and Irache, Santa María de Nájera, San Pedro de Cardeña, Benevivere... and others at Sahagún, Astorga, O Cebreiro and other places. He also brought French churchmen to be their founding superiors: an example was San Lesmes, who in 1070 was a monk at La Chaise-Dieu in the Auvergne, and at royal request went to Burgos, where he founded the church and hospital of San Juan, and built a bridge over the river Arlanzón.

These religious houses consolidated territorial gains and the Christian presence along the frontier, but they also cared for pilgrims. Their existence was meant to encourage - one might even say, make possible - the long journey to the shrine of the apostle James in Galicia. Local initiative was not long in following their examples. Bridge-building and road improvements were undertaken by Santo Domingo de la Calzada and San Juan de Ortega; confraternities and hospitals were founded at strategic points. New towns came into being and older ones expanded with the increasing number of pilgrims and the influx of Frankish pilgrim-settlers. We are reminded of this at places like Villafranca Montes de Oca and Villafranca del Bierzo. All of this meant the Camino Francés - the "French Route" through Navarra, La Rioja and across the *meseta* - became the preferred road, and the coastal way diminished in importance. Even so, the shrine at Oviedo continued to attract pilgrims, so that the road between that city and Leon, with its pilgrim hospital at Santa María de Arbas (also built by Alfonso VI) remained well-travelled in both directions – a way now known as the Camino San Salvador.

During the eleventh century the pilgrimage to Santiago gradually acquired its international dimension. Thanks to court chroniclers and what we might call the monastic 'grapevine', it became better known in the lands beyond Spain. The difficulty of travel to the Holy Land made pilgrimage to the shrine of James the Great a worthy alternative. The result was that the growing fame of the apostolic relics in Galicia shifted what I call the 'conceptual geography' of Christian Europe, creating a new pole in the west, a new focus for popular devotion, that balanced the Byzantine east with its spiritual centre at Jerusalem. For a time, Santiago de Compostela even seemed to rival the pretensions of Rome. Following the Moorish raid of 1000 A.D. that left Alfonso III's church in ruins, Santiago de Compostela was rebuilt. Work began in 1078 on the cathedral we know today, funded by Alfonso VI. Pope Urban II - the same who convened the First Crusade – transferred the see of Iria Flavia to the now more prestigious Santiago de Compostela in 1095.

Then, in the year 1100, the brilliant diplomat Diego Gelmírez became Bishop of Compostela. For the next 40 years he energetically promoted his see, the city and the pilgrimage. Gelmírez was well connected; he had served at the court of the dukes of Aquitaine where he was chancellor to Raymond, a member of the ducal house who was Alfonso VI's son-in-law and count of Galicia. In 1119, Guy de Vienne – Raymond's brother - was elected Pope, and took the name Calixtus II. The way was open for the grant of unique privileges to Compostela. Gelmírez was made archbishop and papal legate in 1120. He lavished funds on the cathedral, creating a magnificent shrine for the relics of St. James the Great.

Archbishop Gelmírez's reign saw the creation of the *Liber Sancti Jacobi* – five books relating to James the Great and the pilgrimage. The collection is prefaced by a letter attributed to Pope Calixtus II, so the entire volume was known as the *Codex Calixtinus*.

The fifth book in the series, the *Pilgrims' Guide*, is often cited as the first traveler's 'guidebook' in the modern sense, and its author as one Aymeric Picaud, a monk of Parthenay-le-Vieux in Poitou (though to some modern scholars, this is now an open question). The work describes, in eleven chapters of varying lengths, the four routes across Gascony, Burgundy, the Auvergne and Provence that fed into the Camino Francés via the Pyrenean passes of Roncesvalles and Somport, and the unified way westwards from Puente la Reina in Navarra. The author describes the terrain and rivers that pilgrims encountered, and supplies a vivid, and frequently prejudiced, foreigner's view of the inhabitants.

The medieval faith in the efficacy of relics, and the passion for their veneration, is reflected in the *Pilgrims' Guide*. The longest chapter is devoted to the relics and miracles of the saints whose shrines were linked by the routes through France, like pearls on a string. Pilgrims could express their devotion, then, at many points during the journey, not only at its destination in far-off Galicia. In the course of many weeks of arduous travel, the prospect of visiting these intermediate shrines kept pilgrims' motivation high. Whatever their reason for 'taking the road' - devotion, the hope of a cure, as penance, or in the fulfilment of a vow – periodic proximity to the relics of the saints helped sustain their resolve.

The hazards of pilgrimage – brigands, accidents, sickness, wild animals – and the uncertainties of travel in unknown regions being what they were, it was natural that pilgrims tended to travel in numbers. Quite apart from resettlement, the pilgrim roads thus became an important factor in the economic development of the areas through which they passed. Royal and church encouragement of the pilgrimage on both sides of the Pyrenees came to include privileges, exemptions from tax or toll, legal provisions designed to protect pilgrims (and sometimes to protect the resident populations *from* pilgrims!) and laws to regulate the commercial activities that arose to cater to their needs.

Given that by the end of the twelfth century, pilgrim numbers had increased to the point where the monastery of Roncesvalles was reportedly feeding some 100,000 pilgrims a year, it is surely not exaggerating to speak of the pilgrimage as a phenomenon that had a profound impact on the society that had produced it. That impact was not only practical, as in some of the ways already mentioned, but cultural, in the exchange and interplay, import and export, of ideas, techniques, skills and modes of artistic expression. With the pilgrims to Santiago, and often as pilgrims themselves, there came French stonemasons, German artisans, Tuscan merchants, Flemish noblemen, English and Burgundian crusaders.... The more educated among them brought, as part of their intellectual baggage, Provencal lyric poetry, Slav legends, Carolingian and Scholastic philosophy, new architectural styles and building methods, and endless music. On the Camino Francés all these influences intermingled and returned to their lands of origin, along with Arab aesthetics and science, medicine and culinary arts. Along the Camino itself, these outside influences contributed to the enhancement of local artistic expression, from Galician-Portuguese troubadour poetry, to the 'pilgrimage churches' and the architectural features of the some of the great cathedrals.

The pilgrimage flourished through the whole medieval period, although actual numbers are hard to determine and must have been subject to the vicissitudes of numerous wars. Mentions of Compostellan Holy Years begin to appear in documents of the late fourteenth and fifteenth centuries, and make it evident that numbers peaked in such years. In much of Europe north of the Alps, and in the British Isles, the Protestant Reformation of the sixteenth century dealt the pilgrimage to Santiago, and the impulse to pilgrimage in general, an all but mortal blow. I have always presumed that, from Spain itself, and from Catholic areas beyond the Pyrenees, pilgrims continued to make their way to Santiago - at least until one shattering and often-overlooked event derailed the pilgrimage for everyone.

That event was the maritime raid on the city of La Coruña by Sir Francis Drake and Sir John Norrys in May 1589. As you can see from any map, La Coruña lies a bare 40 miles from Santiago. There it was feared that Drake intended to capture the relics of the apostle James, the patron of Spain and her empire. In the face of what they believed would be the imminent sack of the city, the Archbishop of Santiago, D. Juan de San Clemente, and two of his most trusted servants opened the tomb, removed the relics, and reburied them where the English would be unable to find them. Unfortunately, they hid them so well that the relics remained effectively 'lost' for the next 300 years.

It must have taken some time for the fact of the empty shrine to become known, but once it *was* known, the arduous pilgrim journey, especially from outside Spain, would have lost much of its inspirational force, although it never entirely died out. It was not until 1879, when a bout of redecoration was taking place in the cathedral, that its renowned historian Antonio López Ferreiro made an educated guess about the reburial that was subsequently confirmed by excavation. Following the comparison of the skull with a jawbone given some centuries before to the cathedral at Pistoia in Italy, the relics were authenticated by Pope Leo XIII in 1884, and replaced under the high altar, where they are today.

Interest in the shrine at Compostela, outside Spain at least, was notably slow to reawaken. Why was this? Obviously, times had changed, and one explanation might be that it had simply fallen through the net of general awareness: most people, even devout Catholics, no longer knew it was there. Another might be Spain's comparative decline after the Spanish-American War and the loss of several of its colonies. A third might be the facts of two World Wars and the Spanish Civil War, and the uncanny coincidence of 20th century Compostellan Holy Years with years of war and their aftermath, or with world exhibitions and trade fairs that commanded greater interest. Not until the Holy Year 1948, a decade after the end of the Civil War and three years after the end of World War II, was the pilgrimage to Santiago and the Year itself widely publicised outside Spain. Special postage stamps were issued, and major art exhibitions mounted. Most notably, the year saw the publication of Vázquez de Parga, Lacarra and Uría Riu's monumental 3-volume study of the pilgrimage, which drew on sources from all the countries and language areas that had once been represented in the crowds that thronged the medieval Camino Francés.

The first significant response came, not surprisingly, from France: the custodian of the four major routes that feed into the *Way* in Spain. In 1950, a small group of historians connected with the National Archives in Paris formed the *Societé des Amis du Chemin de Saint Jacques*. Largely academic in orientation, this group, which included such scholars as Jean Babylon, Jeanne Vieillard and Yves Bottineau, pioneered the formal study of the pilgrimage and produced modern versions of essential texts. Monsignor Henri Branthomme and his companions filmed their pilgrimage to Santiago in 1949 for the French Ministry of Culture. The sight of the Camino and its monuments sparked interest among French television viewers during the 1950's, and a number of hardy French pilgrims walked to Santiago as a result. René Frottier, the Marquis de la Coste Messelière (who was associated with the Amis for more than 40 years, first as Secretary, then President), Henri Roque and others made equestrian pilgrimages, while Jeannine Warcollier provided scholarly and administrative backup to the growing association, then the only provider of information to would-be pilgrims.

The twelve years following the formation of the *Amis* was broken only by a single Holy Year in 1954. Then, with a view to celebrating the next Holy Year in 1965, a Spanish counterpart to the French *Amis* was formed in Estella, a town with strong historic links to the pilgrimage. From the founding of the *Amigos del Camino de Santiago y Centro de Estudios Jacobeos* in 1962, and its designation as a national

Conjunto Historico-Cultural in the same year, we can speak of the beginning of a genuine revival. Those behind the *Amigos* of Estella were interested both in scholarly investigation and in making the pilgrim journey to Santiago once again possible in practical terms. One of them, Francisco Berguete Calleja, a lawyer and local government official, served as President of the Amigos from its formation until shortly before his death in 2000.

In the Holy Year 1965, there were no waymarks, no guidebooks, nowhere to sleep, apart from monastery cells or kindly offered haylofts. Anyone walking the route would have encountered a world in which the memory of the pilgrimage was very much alive, but its physical vestiges little respected. The same farmer who offered a pilgrim food and shelter would have thought nothing of ploughing and planting a crop over the historic thoroughfare.

The *Amigos* performed a notable service when, in 1969, they published the guidebook and maps compiled by one of their members, the musicologist Eusebio Goecoechea Arondo. But while the maps were excellent, the book was far too heavy and detailed to be carried by pilgrims. The solution to this problem came from the other side of the country, where a Galician priest, Father (or 'Don') Elias Valiña Sampedro, having restored the church and village of O Cebreiro, now turned his attention to the pilgrimage route that had been their *raison d'etre*. He had earned his doctorate from the University of Salamanca in 1967, for a thesis on the historical and legal evolution of the Camino Francés as the main pilgrimage route. For the Holy Year 1971, he produced a simple handbook called *Caminos a Compostela*, small enough to fit into a pocket, and containing only the information useful to a pilgrim on foot. This was the forerunner of the much more extensive guide and maps commissioned from him by the Spanish Ministry of Tourism in 1982 (another Holy Year), and reprinted in 1985.

Each of these guidebooks had the effect of increasing the number of pilgrims from Spain and other countries. Meanwhile, also in 1982, Don Elias had undertaken what was probably the single most essential project to revive the Camino Francés : he waymarked it along its entire length, from the border with France in the Pyrenees to the doors of the cathedral in Santiago. Thus came into being the ubiquitous yellow arrow, a symbol he devised, and painted on trees, rocks and buildings, close enough together to foster pilgrim confidence.

The crucial few years in this long renaissance were those between 1982 and 1987, during which Don Elias built up a network of contacts along the Camino who became the founders of regional associations of *Amigos*. He also persuaded many municipal authorities that reclaiming the route, preserving its ancient buildings, and providing shelter for pilgrims were tasks they should properly assume. As a priest, Don Elias could emphasise the Christian obligation inherent in the figure of the pilgrim, while making understood the value to a given locality of a heritage hitherto taken for granted. It was slow work, but ultimately successful. It all helped to create the minimal, but promising, network of practical support that I and some 2,000 other pilgrims found when we made our respective journeys along the Camino Francés during 1986.

The fledgling associations of *Amigos* came together in 1985 to form what I will call for short (since it has a very long name) 'the

THE NEWSLETTER THAT KEPT CAMINO ENTHUSIASTS IN TOUCH: THE FIRST ISSUE OF *BOLETÍN DEL CAMINO*, JULY 1985.

Spanish Federation'. Don Elias was elected its first co-ordinator, and quickly set in motion two far-reaching projects. The first was a modest periodical - the *Boletín del Camino* - which was to be the forerunner of the present-day *Peregrino* magazine. The second was an international conference to address issues of common concern, such as route maintenance, hostels (or *refugios*), the pilgrim passport (or *credencial*), and collaboration between the associations and the

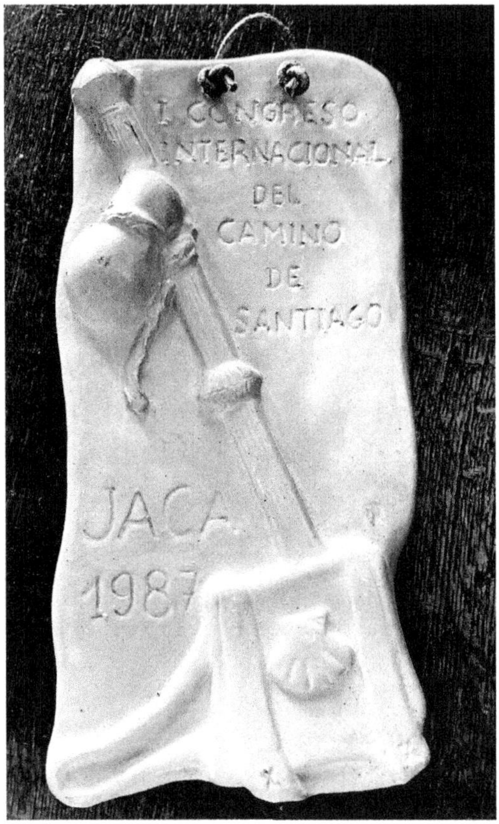

THE SMALL TERRACOTTA PLAQUE GIVEN AS A SOUVENIR TO THOSE WHO ATTENDED THE JACA CONFERENCE

Federation. This conference was held in Jaca, Aragon, in September 1987, and was the first of a series of triennial conferences that continues today. You would perhaps be surprised at how lengthy and convoluted were the debates on some of these matters, and how difficult it sometimes was to achieve a concerted approach, as opposed to a variety of local ones. None the less, such discussion laid the necessary groundwork for the comprehensive support structure that pilgrims enjoy today.

The Jaca conference was also a milestone, in that it was the first forum to which the jacobean associations from outside Spain were invited. There were by now a number of them, in Italy, the United Kingdom, Germany, Belgium and Holland, all founded between 1982 and 1987. In October 1987, a month after Jaca and with Spain a recent member of the European Economic Community, the Council of Europe declared the Camino the first 'European Cultural Itinerary'. This implied protection and promotion, in partnership with the governments of the regions through which the route passed. This began gently, but soon had a major impact, not least visually: the bright blue-and-yellow signs and waymarks erected by the Council of Europe were harbingers of change, initiating the era of the Camino-centred coach tour and the Camino walking holiday.

Following the Jaca conference, when Angel Luis Barreda Ferrer took over as President of the Federation, and into the 1990's, there was a growing tension between the regional associations of *Amigos* and the various interest groups seeking to make economic capital out of the Camino. This was not at all an easy balance to maintain, and by 1991, the year in which the statistical barrier of 10,000 pilgrims was broken, there were many who believed that both the physical integrity of the route and what I will call, for want of a better term, "the pilgrim experience" were being compromised by excessive promotion, especially in Galicia. There were complaints about sections of the ancient pilgrim path being gravelled or paved over, or even eradicated altogether, as roads were widened to take more traffic. There was praise for the waymarking of secondary routes that provided safe alternatives to the roads, for the creation of new *refugios* and the planting of trees. Since the Holy Year 1993, when nearly 100,000 pilgrims on foot, bicycle and horseback received the *compostela*, (the historic certificate of having realised the pilgrimage), the Federation has taken a more proactive role in working with regional governments and with the cathedral in Santiago. But there are now dozens of associations of *Amigos* in Spain, the majority representing areas or pilgrimage routes to Santiago far-removed from the Camino Francés. This has brought its own challenges, but as with so much that is still happening in relation to the pilgrimage, the attempt to meet those challenges has suggested new creative possibilities and avenues.

If there have been identifiable trends since the millennium, they are surely concerned on one hand, with diversification, and on the other, with the preservation and revaluation of 'the pilgrim experience'. These are, I would suggest, the ways of the future, the answer to the second part of our original question of 'Where is it all Going?'.

First comes diversification: the attempt to recover the larger network of routes that pilgrims once took to reach Santiago. In Spain, and to some extent in associations like the Confraternity outside it, this has led to efforts to generate more interest in routes such as the Camino Primitivo and the Camino del Norte, the Via de la Plata, and the routes from the Levant and Portugal. While it is undeniable that in Spain local economic interests are often served by such promotion, and sometimes understandably engage in promotion of their own, the approach of the jacobean associations is that these routes and the monuments on them are eminently worth pilgrims' attention.

Part of their aim is also to alleviate the crowding on the traditional Camino. Some 153,000 pilgrims received the *compostela* in 1999, and nearly 180,000 in 2004 - the overwhelming number of them via the Camino Francés. However comprehensive the infrastructure, numbers like these can strain it. The enduring miracle, to me at least, is that there is so little friction among pilgrims, that local peoples' patience seems to last right to the end of the season, and that pilgrims and locals alike are inexhaustible in their generosity.

Continuing on the theme of diversification, that 'larger network' of historic roads is no longer confined to Spain. It is Europe-wide, just as the medieval one was, and getting wider year by year. The *route de Vézelay* in France and the *Via Francigena* in Italy have enough new infrastructure to make them more viable than they were even a few years ago. The major routes through Switzerland that link up with the *route de Le Puy* farther west are undergoing similar recuperation. Since the fall of the Berlin Wall, scholars have been working on re-establishing the jacobean pilgrimage routes of eastern Europe: the main itineraries that medieval pilgrims followed from the Balkans, Bohemia, Slovenia, Hungary and even Russia before they blended into the throngs marching westwards through France. One such route goes from Prague to Tillyschanz on the German border, and on to Nuremberg and Konstanz. Its recuperation is the fruit of a German-led international effort during the past 8 years, and there is even a Confraternity guide to it. It only awaits its share of pilgrims.

The second priority for the future is the preservation, amidst the numbers and the competing claims for pilgrim custom, of the possibility for silence, contemplation and reflection, shared or individual, and the experience of receiving hospitality. In recent years - and I believe this is a trend that will continue - there has been a welcome return to the appreciation of the pilgrim as a seeker, and a degree of resistance to the commercialisation of the pilgrimage. In many churches along the Camino, pilgrim Masses and blessings are held daily. Some *refugios* offer periods of evening prayer, with a chance to air experiences afterwards. Communities such as the Benedictines in Rabanal and the lay community at Estaing, near Conques, offer pilgrims who ask for it the chance to stay for a few days, a peaceful interlude during which they can weigh up the perplexing issues in their lives. In addition, the impulse that many pilgrims feel on returning home, to 'give something back' to the pilgrimage, has found, since 1991, a formal channel in the wonderful initiative of the *hospitaleros voluntarios*, or voluntary wardens. I am sure that everything about it has been said this week by Jan and Mariluz [in the *Hospitalero* training session at the Conference] - and conveyed by their example, too - but I would just like to emphasise that the feasibility of some of the alternative routes may have much to do with whether there are enough *hospitaleros* to staff the accommodation along them. Not only the Federation, but some of the non-Spanish associations, are always seeking volunteers.

And that brings me to the end of this over-lengthy address. There is an old saying that one's pilgrimage does not end in

The Meson de los Templarios in Villalcazar de Sirga was a traditional pilgrim halt even before the Camino revival of the 1980s. Its owner, Pablo Payo, was popularly known as 'Pablo el Mesonero' for his habit of inviting passing pilgrims to stop for a meal. Here, Don Elias Valiña with Pablo Payo, each proudly wearing a scallop-shell.

Santiago. It begins there, and I am sure that many of us have discovered the truth of that through experience. We return to the lives we left; we are the same, yet not the same; we have gained new perspectives, yet our experience has reaffirmed some fundamentals that we knew all along. The values we come to appreciate on the Camino, and which, I assume, are what have brought us together here today, transcend all the barriers: age, language, race, religion, economic status and educational level. The world - our society - so often seems at odds with those values. To me, and, I suspect, to you also, the pilgrimage to Santiago offers a hopeful vision of how things might be different.

Well, we are in good company. I recently heard a story about Don José María Alonso, the priest at San Juan de Ortega, whom some of you may remember, who has been looking after pilgrims in his particular spot on the Camino for more than 40 years. When Larry Boulting was there in 2002, filming *Within the Way Without*, his crew (which he described to me as 'a pretty irreligious and hard-boiled bunch') was somewhat confused and sceptical about what the Camino was all about. They could understand what the pilgrims were doing, or thought they could, but they didn't understand what a life-long *hospitalero* got out of it. So, over some of the famous garlic soup, they asked Don José María to explain what he and everyone else working on behalf of pilgrims were doing. He, in that characteristic way of his, merely shrugged, smiled and replied 'Oh, ...changing the world - one by one by one.... That's all.'

Father José María Alonso Marroquín of San Juan de Ortega, welcoming pilgrims with bowls of his legendary 'sopa de ajo': bread and garlic soup.

12

Some Pilgrim Memoirs in the Confraternity Library. Presented at *Fin de Sécolo, Fin de Milenio, Finisterre* Vth International Conference of Jacobean Associations, Cee/Corcubión, Galicia, 9-12 October 1999

Creating a library of pilgrimage and Camino-related publications for the Confraternity was one of the earliest priorities of our six founder members back in 1983. They themselves donated the first books, which initially occupied half of a single shelf of a bookcase in the home of one of them.

Seventeen years later, the Stephen Badger Memorial Library, named for the Confraternity's first treasurer and librarian, has become the most important resource in the British Isles for the study of the pilgrimage to Santiago de Compostela and pilgrimage in general. Thanks to the donations of members and the judicious use of a modest annual budget, the Library now comprises some 1,800 volumes* on the history, art and spirituality of the pilgrim roads. Most are in English, but there are also works in French, Spanish, German and Italian. The Confraternity exchanges its own quarterly, *The Bulletin*, for the reviews published by other jacobean associations around the world. It also collects conference proceedings, guidebooks and audio-visual material, and there is a separate Slide Library of photographic images taken and donated by members. The Library is open to anyone by appointment, though borrowing remains the privilege of CSJ members. Books can be sent by post to members who cannot visit the Library in person, and there is an online catalogue.

A number of members have published books about their experience of the Caminos, and these, naturally have found their way into the Library collection. There is also a small section called 'Personal Accounts', which consists of unpublished memoirs written by Confraternity members after completing their pilgrim journeys. The majority are typed on sheets of paper clipped together or held in folders, while others are handwritten, in the journals or notebooks their authors actually carried with them on pilgrimage. It's an interesting group of writings, and I'd like to tell you about a few of them in this brief intervention.

Many, if not most, pilgrims record their thoughts and the events of each day in a diary or journal, but few actually take the additional step of composing a longer narrative on returning home. There are not many who make what they have written, whatever its format, available for others to read. Clearly, from the evidence of those that do, we gather that pilgrimage has led these authors to want to share their experiences with a wider audience than the limited circles of family or friends. They have been able to put aside the usual barriers to self-expression (doubt that anyone will be interested, hesitancy about revealing anything negative, or very personal), so that, ultimately, the desire to communicate has won. Sometimes an introductory comment affirms that the act of ordering their thoughts and making the result available to others has proved exhilarating, or provided new insights that hadn't previously come to mind.

Among the writings I'm referring to, a number stand out as having a common denominator. The journeys described have been made, not only as personal pilgrimages, but also as a means of assisting some worthy cause. These causes are mixed: they can be international or local, and range from the response to a natural disaster to fundraising for a charity, or for a specific project, such as equipping a hospital with a much-needed piece of equipment. The objective may be broad, or closely linked to the pilgrim's personal history. What is notable is that the cause becomes a focal point beyond Santiago, one that incorporates the personal pilgrimage into something bigger, for the benefit of others. The means of achieving it will bring a new kind of petition to the pilgrim's journey: an appeal to like-minded others, in terms of publicity, voluntary help, financial support or any other kind of assistance. As I can testify from experience, this kind of effort involves, touches and benefits many other lives besides the pilgrim's own.

These narratives reveal that sometimes the decision to walk or cycle to Compostela is prompted by painful circumstances. The loss of a friend or family member, or some other life event that has had a radical impact, underlies some of these accounts. One Confraternity member, Judy Foot, playing on words with the title *Foot by Foot,* wrote about walking to Santiago from her farm in the south of England, to raise awareness of the fight against breast cancer after losing a close friend to that disease. Solidarity has provided the motivation for others, such as Paul Graham and Carlos Paternina, as described in *To Santiago by Penny-farthing.* Their cycling pilgrimage from Bordeaux to Santiago, riding a pair of those uncomfortable precursors of the modern bicycle, aimed to help the Spanish MS Society raise awareness of the illness and drum up volunteers. (Later, Paul Graham would do something similar in India for *Help Tibet*, riding from Delhi to Dharamsala, where he met the Dalai Llama, and for *Help the Hospices*, his trusty penny-farthing carrying him from Ramsgate in England to Constanza on the Black Sea.)

The despatches written by Anthony Brunning, a brother of the De La Salle order based in London, provide another such account, published in the *Catholic Herald* newspaper back in the U.K.. Anthony had already walked to Santiago, but when he was appointed to a new position in Rome, he decided to walk there, raising funds for Ethiopian famine relief through the Catholic Fund for Overseas Development (CAFOD). David Baldwin used his Camino experience as the basis for a publication for the CTS Christian Shrines series, while another member, David Longrigg, wrote of the pilgrimage made with his friend, the author and translator John Rutherford, to raise funds to replace the roof of their parish church, a building much venerated in Oxford where they live.

Paul Graham and Carlos Paternina riding their penny-farthings to Santiago in the summer of 1987. Photo Paul Graham and Carlos Paternina

If there is one characteristic of all the writings mentioned so far, it is that they are enriched by an intrepid outlook and the desire to serve. It's clear from what is said of the planning and organisation of these journeys, that such attitudes were in place from the beginning. This differs from the experience of the majority of pilgrims (at least, of those making the journey for the first time), for whom such feelings usually arise during their time on the road, or even later, as part of their arrival in Santiago.

Like all pilgrims, these writers had their ups and downs on the Camino: they found congenial companions, faced physical challenges, had their share of spontaneous, sociable meals and their periods of silent, solitary reflection. What sets their narratives apart from others, and what they have in common, is their identification with the goals they were seeking to achieve. When the going is described as hard and the physical demands as painful or exhausting, there is never a sense that their authors were tempted to give up. Through what they were doing, they were linked to dozens, if not hundreds, of other people, whom they would probably never meet. They aimed to generate thousands of pounds for the organisations they sought to help, without ever having a penny pass through their hands. It's interesting to note that, in contrast to the way that highly publicized celebrity fundraising campaigns and 'sponsored' events are carried out, these pilgrims have not sought or received any material recompense, not even to cover their own expenses, from the organisations they seek to assist. Each has simply turned his or her pilgrimage into a gift.

All of these memoirs engage and even inspire the reader, but if I had to choose one as outstanding, it would be Major Tim O'Neill McCoy's *With Cross and Sword.* Tim McCoy was a retired businessman with a distinguished earlier career in the British army. He was Secretary of the U.K.'s Wine and Spirits promotional board, and a senior instructor for the Royal Yachting Association. In the autumn of 1993, he survived a violent robbery in Central London. After five days in a coma and two years of rehabilitation, he was left with permanent brain injuries that included damage to his sense of balance, and the loss of sight in one eye that from then on required him to wear an eye-patch. He could no longer walk without a sturdy stave, nor without pain. His Catholic faith, and his gratitude to the medical staff of Stoke Mandeville hospital, strengthened him during his difficult transition back to independent living. Inspired by a book about walking to Santiago de Compostela, he decided to make the pilgrimage himself, offering it in support of SCOPE, the British association that assists people with brain damage. It was also, as he later described it, 'a journey in search of what remained of the person he had once been, and discovery of who he had become'.

The text that Tim wrote on completing his pilgrimage from Chartres to Compostela, a distance of some 1600 kilometres, spares the reader nothing of his mental and physical struggle. Not only did he do battle with constant pain and the elements, but also with inward doubt, frequent rejection on account of his appearance, and the forced apprenticeship of his new limitations. It is, none the less, a moving and inspiring account. The description of his arrival in Santiago, with a case of pneumonia that landed him in hospital, but also with the conviction that the Apostle was summoning him to a life of service, confirms yet again the transforming and healing effect of walking the Camino. It was not only SCOPE that benefited from Tim's pilgrimage, but everyone he worked with to achieve his aim, and many of the fellow-pilgrims he met along the way. In a category of writing that is already very special, this narrative, to me, has pride of place.

(*) In 2022, 7000 volumes

AFTERWORD
A Labyrinth in a Quiet Garden

Twenty-four years after arriving in Santiago de Compostela as a pilgrim, I bought a stone house only steps from the route I'd walked in 1986. None of my new neighbours could tell me exactly how old the house was, but they recalled that it had once been known as 'la Casa del Rojo' after the Republican who had owned it before the Civil War. Its legal name, the one on the deeds, was 'la Casa del Chao' or 'the house by the hill' but nobody ever called it that. Its name had disappeared with 'el Rojo', along with the fields and woodland that had once belonged to it. Since the 1950s the house had changed hands half a dozen times.

The Spanish couple who sold it to me had bought it as a semi-ruin, and restored it lovingly. They'd also created a garden in the space around it, adding dozens of ornamental trees to the native ash, rowan, beech, hazel, oak, holly and elder already there. From an altitude of 1,200 metres, the view of the surrounding countryside was astonishing, but equally so were the beds of hydrangeas that bordered the house on two sides. My predecessors had a passion for them, and drove all over Galicia, Asturias and Cantabria in search of varieties that could survive and thrive in the extreme climate of Lugo's *Alta Montaña*. Now there were metre-high 'mopheads' and 'lacecaps' in colours ranging from deep purple, indigo and burgundy to the palest pink and blue, some flowering in such abundance that their leaves were all but hidden, some with foliage as dark as wine.

The view, the trees and the hydrangeas were the predominant features of the garden, but there was also a lot of grass – or rather, a huge expanse of rough mountain pasture, bounded by a dry-stone wall. Here was a space big enough to realise an idea that had been in the back of my mind for years: creating a replica of the labyrinth of Chartres cathedral, from which I'd started my pilgrimage to Compostela all those years ago. By the time a third summer rolled around, I felt the time was right to begin. Luckily the previous owners had passed on the name of their gardener, Francisco (Paco) Garcia, whose help I enlisted in turning a mole-infested, weedy field into something very different.

As so often is the case, the preparatory stage was the toughest. I explained the idea to a neighbour, who agreed to plough up and level the designated area. (Years later, by which time the labyrinth had actually begun to look like something, he admitted he'd thought I was crazy.) Removing wheelbarrow-loads of rocks from the newly exposed surface, then compacting it, took days. Paco, as it happened, coached young football teams when he wasn't gardening, and had access to one of those machines that chalks lines on a pitch. It proved invaluable when the time came to mark out the image of the Chartres labyrinth I'd downloaded from the internet, and carefully measured out using stakes and string.

'La Casa del Laberinto' with the labyrinth in the foreground.
Photo José Luis Neira Fernández

Then it was time to walk the path between the lines, paying particular attention to the gaps indicating turns and the short lines creating dead ends. I insisted that we each walk it twice, noting any points of doubt. Only then did I arrange delivery of the 1,800 plants I had ordered. They were a miniature variety of box, *Buxus sempervirens 'Suffruticosa'*, and on arrival were each the size of my index finger. We spent back-breaking days planting them 15 inches apart along the white lines that made up the labyrinth's eleven circles and flower-shaped central space. I must admit to fearing for them, so small and spindly did they appear. Paco suggested that they'd need copious watering until they became established. Luckily, here in La Laguna the water comes from a mountain spring that has never been known to fail, even in the hottest and driest conditions. I spent many a long, peaceful summer evening watering the little plants, as the valley below fell into shadow and the stars emerged, one by one.

By the end of their first season the box plants were noticeably sturdier, but it took three years for them to develop enough side growth to form a low hedge. By then I'd transplanted some lavender bushes to create an approach to the entrance to the labyrinth. In its fourth summer, fed up with trying to keep its paths reasonably free of weeds, I ordered a truckload of pinkish stones, slightly larger and much prettier than gravel, to discourage them. A friend donated a bench, to rest on after completing the labyrinthine journey.

In 2015, I registered the garden as one of more than 300 around the world belonging to the Quiet Garden Movement. It was the first – and for several years, the only – Quiet Garden in Spain, and brought to nineteen the number of countries in which such gardens exist. The principle is simple, defined by the movement's founder, the Reverend Philip Roderick, in the early 1990s, as places that provide a respite from busy lives, places of encounter – with God, nature, silence, or whatever it is that visitors to them seek. Owners make their gardens freely available to others for quiet time and reflection, and for gatherings centred on prayer, creative expression and the experience of nature. Today these gardens can be found in urban settings and country villages; there are large ones, small ones, and increasingly, institutional ones belonging to schools, hospitals,

THE AUTHOR, CLEARLY BETTER WITH WORDS
THAN AT SIGN-PAINTING.
PHOTO KIM NARENKIVICIUS

churches and prisons. The people who visit mine range from my neighbours' grandchildren, who come to play in it, to pilgrims who make a detour from the Camino Francés to walk it, local people who bring family members or friends to see it, and tourists who have somehow heard of it. One of the unforeseen results of registering it has been that my house has once again acquired a name. As 'La Casa del Laberinto' (accurate, if not original), it appears on the Quiet Gardens Association website: my small thank-offering to Galicia, the Camino and life in general.

That last comment is a partial answer to anyone curious about why I would want to replicate the Chartres labyrinth in a Galician hamlet. It can be only partial, because the answer isn't as simple as the question, which is one I've been asked many times - but I will have a go.

I'd visited Chartres and walked its famous labyrinth long before I heard of the pilgrimage to Santiago de Compostela, yet the similarity between the two exercises did not strike me until I had actually given St. James his hug and returned home. Both trajectories symbolise, to me, the human journey of life with all its challenges and hard-won understanding. The pilgrim's arrival at the goal, whether this be a shrine or the centre of a labyrinth, is at the same time the first step of the journey back into the world, where 'ordinary' life awaits the transforming power of the pilgrim's revised perception of it. Making the labyrinth in La Laguna also seemed right, and timely. As one who rejoices in the abundance and generosity of nature, I experience the garden as a kind of open-air cathedral, a setting so uplifting in itself as to be a fitting context for the labyrinth. And if not here and now, then where, and when?

This isn't the place to summarise a lot of history available elsewhere, but it is worth clarifying the difference between labyrinths and mazes, especially because, in Spanish, there is no such distinction: the word 'laberinto' is used for both. European mazes usually date from the renaissance, and were largely devised to amuse, as virtuoso works of garden design in which people could play at being lost. A maze may or may not have a centre, but its many paths, some of which bifurcate or intersect or terminate in dead ends, make it a giant puzzle. Finding the way out of a maze is meant to be challenging, as at

WALKING THE LABYRINTH AT CHARTRES CATHEDRAL

PHOTO COURTESY OF WIKIMEDIA CREATIVE COMMONS

the famous one at Hampton Court, where wardens frequently rescue visitors who have been wandering for hours.

Labyrinths, on the other hand, date from ancient times. The mythical one at Knossos in Crete was the lair of the minotaur - half-man, half-bull - slain by the hero Theseus. The hero's journey is Everyone's, in the sense that it represents the human quest for self-mastery in facing psychic as well as physical dangers. Given that Theseus needed the thread supplied by Ariadne to find his way out of the Cretan labyrinth, we may deduce that it was really a maze, designed to confuse and entrap. 'Classical' labyrinths, in contrast, are 'unicursal' in having only one path leading to a centre, which when walked in reverse leads back to the entrance. An interesting illustration of one, apparently taken from a Roman signet ring, depicts a centaur (standing in for the minotaur, perhaps?) in its central space, and appears in a 17th century manuscript entitled *Gemme Antiche*, now in the Laurentian Library in Florence.

'Classical' labyrinths, with varying numbers of circles, seem to have been universal symbols of search, discovery and reintegration produced by many cultures around the world. Here in Galicia, as in Spain's Basque country, bronze-age depictions survive as petroglyphs.

Specifically Christian labyrinths of the 'Classical' type, like the one at Chartres, are medieval, and usually consist of eleven rounds surrounding a six-lobed central space, though many, both ancient and modern, have only seven. The walker is required to makes elaborate twists and turns on the way to the centre, and having reached it, to navigate the same path in reverse, until he finds himself back where he started.

It is thus impossible to get lost in a cathedral labyrinth such as the one at Chartres. On countless occasions I've joked with visitors to the garden expecting to find a maze, that 'you lose yourself in one of those, but you find yourself in this one'. This hints at the main reason why I wanted to recreate the Chartres labyrinth here: it reiterates the essential message of the Camino. The labyrinth design is simple, yet profoundly meaningful, thanks to the sacred geometry that finds expression in every aspect of the cathedral itself. This geometry,

The Morgor petroglyphs in Galicia are estimated to be between three and five thousand years old.
photo Galicia Tourist Office

reflected in the visual shorthand of the labyrinth, reveals to the pilgrim seeker the same message as does the 'spiritual geography' of the Camino. Both paths lead to a physical destination, but also to an interior one, which is the simple, but profound, revelation that unconditional love sustains the world.

Such an insight is a gift, irrespective of the condition or merit of the person who receives it, as the receiver knows all too well. This is not to suggest that the Camino, or a labyrinth in a cathedral, have a monopoly on such insights. There are pilgrimage routes around the world, associated with all the great religions, that give rise to them, and there are secular routes (such as the Appalachian

Trail or the Pennine Way), along which the kindness shown to walkers parallels the hospitality offered to pilgrims on the Caminos. In truth, the experiences conducive to inward growth and illumination are innumerable. They need not be physical, and can sometimes be painful, such as the inner journeys made through psychoanalysis, or forced upon people by tragic life events. What they have in common is that the insight gained is not 'forgettable' without grave interior dishonesty. It must be lived out – or perhaps a better term might be 'loved out'. It goes without saying that in attempting this, humility and gratitude are constant companions.

The walking pilgrim's openness to encounter owes much to the fact that walking long distances is a category of travel all its own. Weeks and even months on the road calm the mind and allow it to reconnect with the physical self, producing a heightened sense of awareness and emotional receptivity. Within the framework of the physical journey, and despite the many differences among individual pilgrims, the experience of receiving hospitality is for each one both personal and shared. For once, the ideal of fraternity is operative, rather than merely conceptual. All faiths teach the duty of charity, but hospitality, even when it involves extending charity, adds another dimension to it. Charity seeks to relieve suffering, or to fill some basic material need. Hospitality regards its recipients, without distinction, as brothers, friends or guests. The person who receives charity may not necessarily feel welcomed or validated by it, but the person who receives hospitality automatically feels welcomed and validated, because being generously received and cared for is what defines the term.

The traditional welcome given to strangers (the *philoxenia* of ancient Greece, that later combined with Christian teaching on charity throughout the Mediterranean world), was part of what sustained the pilgrimage to Compostela through the centuries, and was an essential factor in its modern revival. The duty of charity was universally recognised in Spain's largely Catholic culture (and in the half-century after the Civil War, no-one lacked opportunities to act on it) but so too, given the genial Spanish temperament, was the importance accorded to hospitality. People living along the pilgrim routes in the 1940s were accustomed to destitute folk begging from door to door, from whom, as I have it on good report, pilgrims were often indistinguishable. Not that there were many pilgrims, but the tradition of inviting them to a bowl of soup or letting them sleep in the hayloft remained part of the way of life. In a country where families were often large, and usually 'extended', in which the ties of blood relationship remained strong through the generations, and links to the ancestral village and homestead enabled those who lived elsewhere to return in summer, people were used to large gatherings and to laying an extra place at the table. The old refrain '*donde comen dos, comen tres*' (roughly translatable as 'where two can eat, there's enough for three') sums up a generous, gregarious approach to life that helped make it possible for a few intrepid pilgrims to travel the Caminos in the era before there were places to stay, eat or buy provisions.

In 1971, when Elias Valiña produced his modest guide to the Camino Francès, *Caminos a Compostela*, his belief in the possibility of reviving the pilgrimage was often met with indifference by officialdom along the route. All he had to counter this were two somewhat intangible assets. One was his detailed knowledge of the route, gained through the research for his doctoral thesis, which concentrated on the evolution of the legal framework that defined the medieval thoroughfare and ensured the safety of pilgrims. The other was his confidence in the popular tradition of hospitality. For the next decade and beyond, from the Pyrenees to rural Galicia, he persuaded his fellow-parish priests to provide 'refugio', or sleeping space for pilgrims, and local historians to identify the vestiges of the pilgrimage in their areas. It was hard to get farmers to cease planting over the ancient path, and harder still to talk small town mayors into preserving ruins that had once been pilgrim hospitals, but in time, he won them over. In all this, the emphasis was on how reviving the Camino could strengthen cultural identity, and in time, bring economic benefits – an important consideration in poor, rural areas of Spain.

Just as importantly, though this would take time to become apparent, he sought out villagers all along the Camino Francés, for whom the occasional passing pilgrims had always been part of life. By recognising their efforts and introducing such people to one another, he created a chain of potential support for the pilgrims he was convinced would come, once the existence of such support could be made known. Some of these people, or their family members, later became the cornerstones of associations of 'Amigos del Camino'. Some banded together to rehabilitate a shed or garage as 'refugio'. Some reclaimed all-but-forgotten springs, and had the water tested for potability. Others set up cairns or crosses as waymarking. Each of these small practical initiatives was a step in reaffirming the existence of the pilgrimage, and an encouraging sign that walking or cycling or riding a horse along the Camino was becoming viable.

If the opening of the *Hospederia de San Giraldo O Cebreiro* in 1966 had been a milestone, *Caminos a Compostela* was another. From 1971, a restored *palloza* became a 'refugio', which Elias kept amply supplied with fresh straw bedding. Nights spent in this austere but atmospheric shelter are recalled to this day by the pilgrims of the 1970s and 80s. So are the memories of Elias himself, inviting pilgrims over to the *Hospederia* for suppers of tortilla and nourishing soup before they settled down next to the fireplace to swap stories. As members of his family recall, no time of day or night was too early or too late to attend to pilgrims. Meals were prepared for them whenever they arrived, sometimes by Elias himself, who was adept at creating some sustaining dish from whatever came to hand at midnight. If their clothes were wet, the *Hospederia*'s radiators were cleared to dry them. Any stalwarts travelling the Camino in winter were invited to sleep on the floor of its dining room, warmed by log fires in the big *chimenea*. (From 1989 I have my own memories of this – not because I slept there, but because I sometimes ferreted out a blanket for someone who did, and for some of the conversations I had with pilgrims glad of a late-night ear.) There were few autumn or winter pilgrims back then (precisely five passed through between 12 October, the feast of *El Pilar*, and Christmas day in 1989), but the few there were might find themselves, especially on Saturday evenings, invited to dine with the local doctor or vet on night duty, a priest from Lugo attending some nearby parish, men going on shift at the zinc mine at Rubiales, a few kilometres away, or with all of the above, at the long table that ran along one wall of the dining room.

The point of all this is that the kinds of attention I have described were aimed at making pilgrims feel welcomed and the fact of their making the pilgrimage valued. None of it cost the pilgrim much, if anything, in monetary terms, but what they gained was priceless. They were treated as intimates, not strangers, and the example set by Elias and his family in so treating them had immense repercussions for the Caminos. I write here of one such result which I know first-hand, since I was present at the meeting when Walter Ivens presented to the committee of the Confraternity of Saint James his proposal for what would become Refugio Gaucelmo in Rabanal del Camino. He read, and I quote, 'We could help to convert, with care, some of the old houses into a pilgrims' hostel like the amenities and atmosphere at O Cebreiro'.

That project, as I've described elsewhere in this book, came to fruition through the individual donations of our members, who shared Walter's dream of 'giving back' to the Camino a little of what each felt that he or she had received from it. That the albergue would function on a 'donativo' basis was a foregone conclusion, since we have always believed that the effect this has on travellers – especially on those from 'First World' countries, where everything has its price tag - of being treated as friends and guests, solely and precisely because they are pilgrims, far outweighs whatever else we might offer them.. This does not mean that Refugio Gaucelmo is 'free'. It does not charge, but it invites a contribution, explaining that those contributions provide

THE DONATIVOS BOX AT REFUGIO GAUCELMO.
SEE PP. 149-150 FOR THE STORY OF HOW IT WAS MADE.

fellow pilgrims' afternoon teas and breakfasts, as well as the cleaning materials that ensure the albergue's comfort and cleanliness. Pilgrims are 'free' in the sense that each decides whether and how much to contribute – and although, strictly speaking, there is no obligation to leave a monetary donation, there are plenty of ways to help out, if someone is short of funds. The first two pilgrims ever to stay in the refuge, back in 1991, walked through the door asking 'What can we do to help?', and as Joe May, the CSJ member who put brooms into their hands later said, 'If that doesn't epitomise the spirit of the Camino, I don't know what does'.

The shift in perspective brought about by disinterested generosity can sometimes be so extreme as to move pilgrims to tears. I have met so many over the years who report its impact on them, in so many words, as 'it made me see the world differently' that I no longer have any hesitation about affirming this. When they carry that shift in world view back into their daily lives, and into society at large, we can understand what Jose Maria Alonso, the parish priest of San Juan de Ortega, meant when he said that receiving pilgrims and sitting them down for bowls of his famous garlic soup, day after day, year after year, was 'changing the world, one by one by one...'. As someone who devoted much of his life, not just to receiving pilgrims, but also to listening to them, he knew what he was talking about.

That is why it is so important that the traditional *albergues de donativo*, where pilgrims receive hospitality and can actively collaborate in their own and others' stay, are not pressured out of existence. They are not just reflections of the Camino's past, though they certainly are that. They also provide experiences conducive to inward change, and ultimately, to societal change, in ways that purely monetary transactions do not. Pilgrims do not lack opportunities for the latter, and indeed, many may prefer them, but there should also be a place on the Caminos for those who seek

Lavender borders the path leading to the labyrinth.
photo Kim Narenkivicius

the historic and human resonance of traditional hospitality. Striving to make the pilgrimage more inclusive and accessible makes little sense if economic factors become obstacles in their turn. There must be space and a place for all, for a plurality of ways and means, as there has always been, down the centuries.

Seven years on (a mere blip in Camino terms) from when it was planted, the outline of the labyrinth is a bushy, solid hedge that stands knee-high. I walk those eleven circles myself sometimes, and reflect on the path of life they represent – our onward journey included.

ACKNOWLEDGMENTS

I'm proud that *Waybread* will bear the imprint of Peaceable Publishing. I want to thank Rebekah Scott, not just for sharing her imprimatur, but for spotting the potential value of such a book at what we both see as a critical time for the Caminos.

I also want to thank Kim Narenkivicius for her work as designer, and her editorial and technical help in bringing the book to fruition. We are all deeply grateful to José Luis Neira Fernández, who has kindly allowed us to use his photograph of my house and garden here in La Laguna as a jacket illustration. I would also like to thank those whose photographs appear in the book alongside my own and those belonging to the Lopez and Valiña families.

The author, delighted at meeting Ursula Martin, who was walking from Kyiv to Santiago and stopped in O Cebreiro on 15 February 2021.
photo Ursula Martin

ABOUT THE AUTHOR

LAURIE DENNETT was born in Toronto and grew up in Agincourt, Ontario, Canada. She studied history at the University of Toronto, McMaster University in Hamilton, and the University of St Andrews, Scotland. As an independent historian in the City of London she was the author of eight commissioned histories, including those of Prudential, Slaughter and May and the Institute of Actuaries.

In 1986 she walked from Chartres, France, to Santiago de Compostela in aid of MS research funding. The 1987 memoir of her pilgrimage, *A Hug For The Apostle,* sold out in eight months and became a Camino classic. Later pilgrimages, also undertaken to raise awareness and funds for Multiple Sclerosis research, took her from London to Rome (1989) and Canterbury to Jerusalem (1992). Laurie chaired Britain's Confraternity of Saint James from 1995 to 2003. She now lives near O Cebreiro in Galicia, where she hosts a 'Quiet Garden' that includes a replica of the Chartres cathedral labyrinth. Her most recent book was *An American Princess: The Remarkable Life of Marguerite Chapin Caetani* (McGill-Queen's University Press, 2016). A slightly revised, illustrated edition of *A Hug For The Apostle* was published by Words Indeed of Toronto in 2019.

www.waybread.org

The Road to Santiago, one of the great roads of Europe and of the world for longer than a millennium, links nations in ways that no bureaucracy ever can. It exists for and because of a spiritual dimension to human life that transcends the barriers of language and creed. It holds out a personal goal to all. In a troubled world, it remains a symbol of international goodwill and a testament to the survival of the values that foster it.

– *From the author's notebook, following a conference on the Camino de Santiago, Cologne, March 1987*

PHOTO ANTONIO MAESO JOANA

Printed in Great Britain
by Amazon

22685157R00173